WRITER WRITER

THE WRITER'S GUIDE
TO GETTING PUBLISHED

Practical books that inspire

The Writer's Guide to Research
*An invaluable guide to gathering material for
features, novels and non-fiction books*

Writer's Guide to Copyright and Law
Get your full financial reward and steer clear of legal pitfalls

Write & Sell Your Novel
The beginner's guide to writing for publication

Writing a Children's Book
How to write for children and get published

The Internet Guide for Writers
Use the Internet for writing, research and information

How To Books
3 Newtec Place, Magdalen Road,
Oxford OX4 1RE, United Kingdom
E-mail: info@howtobooks.co.uk
http://www.howtobooks.co.uk

The Writer's Guide to Getting Published

Chriss McCallum

5th edition

howtobooks

Published by How To Books Ltd,
3 Newtec Place, Magdalen Road
Oxford OX4 1RE United Kingdom.
Tel: (01865) 793806. Fax: (01865) 248780.
email: info@howtobooks.co.uk
http://www.howtobooks.co.uk

British Library Cataloguing in Publication Data
A catalogue record for this book is available from the British Library

Cover design by Baseline Arts Ltd, Oxford
Produced for How To Books by Deer Park Productions
Typeset by PDQ Typesetting, Newcastle-under-Lyme, Staffs.
Printed and bound in Great Britain by Bell & Bain Ltd, Glasgow

NOTE: The material contained in this book is set out in good faith for general guidance and no liability
can be accepted for loss or expense incurred as a result of relying in particular circumstances on
statements made in the book. The laws and regulations are complex and liable to change, and readers
should check the current position with the relevant authorities before making personal arrangements.

ISBN: 1 85703 877 0

Contents

List of illustrations

Preface to the Fifth Edition

You want to get published, so where do you start? In today's volatile and highly competitive publishing world, you need a guide to show you how to give yourself the best chance of success. This book is your guide. Follow its advice and you'll save yourself a lot of time, money and frustration.

The writers who get their work published are not necessarily the most brilliant. They are writers who provide what editors and publishers want. Being a successful writer means balancing your individuality and enthusiasm with your writing and selling skills. It means:

- adopting a professional attitude from the start
- writing as well as you can in your chosen field
- giving editors what they want, not what you think they should want
- presenting your work as editors like to see it
- developing a mutually profitable relationship with a publisher.

My aim is to show you how to get *your* work published. Believe me, and believe in yourself.

ACKNOWLEDGEMENTS

My thanks to these kind people who gave me permission to include copyright material: Mike Pattinson, Peggy Poole, Jean Sergeant, D C Thomson & Co Ltd, and Steve Wetton.

AUTHOR'S NOTE

Editors and publishers, like writers, spring from both sexes. If anyone can invent a workable device to convey that fact neatly and without the awkward use of 'he or she', 'he/she', '(s)he' and the like, I'll be glad to hear from you. In the meantime, please read 'he', 'him' and 'his' throughout this text as embracing both men and women. No sexism is intended. After all, despite my slightly androgynous name, I am a woman.

Chriss McCallum

Getting Started

Writing for publication is a fiercely competitive business. By accepting that fact at the outset, you'll approach your writing and the business of selling it in the best way and with the best chance of success.

In this chapter:

◆ what it takes to become a published writer
◆ basic equipment
◆ building your writer's reference library
◆ finding inspiration and support.

BEFORE YOU STEP IN

The publishing business today is a buyer's market. Don't underestimate what that means. The acceptance rate for unsolicited novel manuscripts, for instance, is about one in two thousand – very long odds. But you *can* shorten them. You can:

◆ Get to know how the publishing business works.

◆ Learn how to identify, analyse and approach your target markets.

◆ Understand why you have to offer editors what they want, not what you think they *should* want.

◆ Learn how to develop a mutually profitable professional relationship with the editors you want to do business with.

The writing world is full of hopeful authors who will never see a word of theirs in print because they don't – or won't – understand the need to work at both the craft of writing and the art of selling.

There's no secret recipe, no magic formula. Success requires work – and staying power. Legions of writers bombard editorial offices with manuscripts that are unstructured, badly written and all too often directed to the wrong market anyway. They are amazed and upset when their submissions boomerang home trailing rejection slips. Many give up in despair and disillusionment.

You can succeed where these writers fail. You can learn:

- The basic techniques of good writing.

- How to structure your writing.

- How to choose and use language effectively.

- How to communicate your thoughts clearly, without muddle or ambiguity.

- How to capture and hold your reader's interest.

- How to revise and rewrite, and rewrite again until your work is as good as you can make it.

You'll find references throughout the following chapters to books, magazines, courses, associations, services and information sources that will help you master the craft of writing and develop the skills you need to become a published writer. To avoid unnecessary repetition, details are given in the appendices – titles, names, addresses, telephone numbers, e-mail and website addresses.

You'll also find advice and encouragement, and the occasional caution, all designed to help you achieve your goal.

Take yourself seriously...
You might not find it easy to think of yourself as a serious writer when you're just starting out. You'll agonise about your chances of success, and wake up in the small hours nagged by doubt. Take comfort. You're not alone – and beginners who are *too* sure of themselves tend to trip over their own egos.

Have confidence in your capacity to learn. Approach your writing from the start in a professional manner. After all, if you don't believe in your ability, how can you expect to convince other people.

... and be taken seriously
The book aims to help you build your confidence, judgement and credibility. It will also:

◆ Give you a working knowledge of the writing business and its accepted practices and conventions, to help you avoid many of the pitfalls that commonly beset the inexperienced writer.

◆ Help you decide where you want to start. Even if you've already chosen your field (or if your field has chosen you, as often happens) don't dismiss other options altogether. You might see a better starting point, or want to branch out later.

Common sense
Too many new writers are drawn to one of two extreme attitudes:

◆ There's the writer who devours all the advice he can get hold of, treating every word as gospel. He tears himself apart trying to adapt his style, approach, technique, marketing strategy, because the advice he's reading this week contradicts what he read last week. He has no faith in his own judgement, and makes no effort to develop any.

♦ The opposite type refuses to consider *any* advice or help from anyone. He drives editors to distraction with his lack of common sense. He shoots off book-length stories to tiny magazines, single poems to book publishers, erudite essays to mass-market magazines....

WISE WORDS

Learn the business, use your common sense, and you won't create problems where none need exist.

Here, then, are a few basic common-sense Dos and Don'ts to bear in mind as you read:

1. *Do* study the techniques of good, clear writing, but *don't* submerge your individuality.

2. *Do* study your markets so you send them material that is suitable, but *don't* copy their style and content so closely that you sacrifice every trace of originality.

3. *Do* be courteous and businesslike in all your dealings with editors, but *don't* regard them either as enemies or gods. They're not 'anti' new writers, or unapproachable, or infallible, or exalted – they're human beings with problems and prejudices, mortgages and falling hair, just like the rest of us.

4. *Do* work at cultivating your own judgement, but *don't* try to defy the conventions before you understand them.

5. And, above all, *do* write. *Don't* just think or talk or read or dream about writing. *Do it.*

BASIC EQUIPMENT

In theory, all you need is a pen and a pad of paper. In practice, it isn't that simple. Editors won't read handwritten scripts. You have to be able to present your work in the form of a typescript. Though it looks like a contradiction in terms, this is usually called a manuscript (abbreviation 'ms', plural 'mss').

Unless you're rich, you'll need to prepare your ms yourself. (Rates for professional word processing are at least £3 per 1,000 words plus extra for hard copies, of which you'll need at least two – one to send out and one to keep safe in your files – plus a copy on disk.) Even a short novel could cost £300–£400, almost enough to buy a computer package.

Learn to touch type, so you can concentrate on your writing, not on what your fingers are doing. Take a course or buy Ann Dobson's book *Touch Typing in Ten Hours*.

You'll need:

- Pens and pocket-sized notebooks, so you can jot down ideas instantly. Keep one by your bed, too, to capture (in the dark if necessary) those verge-of-sleep flashes of brilliance. They'll be lost by morning if you don't. (A pocket tape recorder is even better.) Ideas, impressions, words, phrases, overheard anecdotes – they can slip away forever if you don't pin them down.

- Plain white A4 (11.6 × 8.2 inches) paper, 80 gsm (grammes per square metre) weight, for manuscripts. (Don't waste this on notes or drafts – use unwanted flyers and the like, or get cheap notepads from cut-price stationery shops.)

- A decent printer. If you're still using a typewriter, renew the ribbon well before the print begins to look faded. Don't bother making carbon copies – they're no longer acceptable. Make clean sharp photocopies, and keep the original for additional copies. Use only *black* ink cartridges or ribbons.

- Plain white DL size (9 × 4.5 inches) business envelopes.

- C5 (9 × 6.5 inches) envelopes to hold A4 sheets folded once.

- A4 envelopes, to hold mss of more than four pages without folding.

> **TIP**
>
> Mail order companies and office supply shops are cheaper than high street shops. White A4 80 gsm copier paper is perfectly acceptable for manuscripts.

You can get your writing career off the ground with clean error-free typescripts, but more and more magazines and book publishers now require work supplied on disk along with hard copy. You're also disadvantaged if you can't send and receive e-mail.

With a computer you can:

> **TIP**
>
> Buy a computer as soon as you can.

- Edit your work without retyping whole pages.

- Electronically store copies of everything you write.

- Print copies of your writing as and when you need them.

- Copy your work on to computer disks.

- Send files of your work electronically anywhere in the world.

- Send query letters by e-mail.

- Respond to editors' questions in minutes rather than days.

- Find information via the Internet.

Every successful writer works in his or her own way. Fay Weldon, interviewed on Channel 4, declared that if the day ever comes when she's required to write on a machine she'll stop writing. She writes with a pen and pad, and pays someone else to prepare her mss. That's fine, if you can afford the luxury.

THE GOLDEN RULE

Always back up your work on to a separate disk at the end of every work session. Ideally, make copies on two disks and keep one on other premises, perhaps in your shed or garage, in case of – Heaven forbid – fire or burglary.

Make backing up an unbreakable habit. Writers have lost weeks or even years of work because they haven't bothered to take this basic precaution.

BUILDING YOUR REFERENCE LIBRARY
Buy these books – you'll use them a lot:

- A big fat dictionary. *Chambers Dictionary* is excellent.

- The *latest* edition of the *Writers' & Artists' Yearbook* or *The Writer's Handbook*. Buy both if you can afford to. These annual directories list book, magazine and newspaper publishers and what they want from writers, plus radio, stage and TV markets. The *Yearbook* gives lots of advice about writing and getting published, agents, associations, services, tax liabilities, rights, copyright and so on. The *Handbook* lists fewer outlets than the *Yearbook* but gives more details about those it does include, and covers more radio, TV and stage outlets.

- *The Oxford Dictionary for Writers & Editors.* For difficult spellings and usage, many proper names, capitalisation, abbreviations, foreign words and phrases.

- A concise encyclopedia, like the annual *Pears Cyclopedia.*

- *Roget's Thesaurus*, which lists synonyms for almost every word in the English language. Marvellous for finding just the right word – but don't get addicted to it.

Note: Other recommended books are listed in appropriate chapters throughout the book.

INFORMATION SOURCES

Using the public library

You'll probably use the library a good deal, so it's worth noting the main category divisions of the Dewey Decimal Classification System, which is used in most UK libraries. The category numbers are shown on the shelves, and it saves time if you know where to start looking:

000 General works
100 Philosophy
200 Religion
300 Social sciences
400 Languages
500 Science
600 Technology
700 The arts and recreations
800 Literature
900 Geography, biography and history.

Out of print books and books on your special subject

The monthly *Book and Magazine Collector* lists books 'For Sale' and 'Wanted'. Although mainly meant for book dealers and collectors, it's useful for writers, too. Many book dealers specialise, and you can ask to be put on the mailing lists of those who deal in books relevant to your particular interests. You can advertise for books yourself, too. The magazine also carries ads for book-finding services.

Writers' magazines

There are magazines specially produced for writers. They print advice, news, reviews, competition notices, information on what's happening on the writing scene, plus author interviews and articles on the craft and business of writing and getting published.

Most writers' magazines are sold on subscription, but two are stocked by larger newsagents. These are:

◆ *Writers' Forum*, published ten times a year and also sold on subscription. Glossy and colourful, it covers all aspects of writing and getting published, with numerous ads of interest to writers at all levels. *Writers' Forum* also runs regular prose and poetry competitions and publishes successful short stories and poems from these competitions.

◆ *Writing Magazine*, the bi-monthly glossy 'big sister' of the monthly subscription title *Writers' News* (see below). *Writing Magazine* carries articles and interviews encouraging both the hobby writer and the would-be professional, with market information, competitions, and a multitude of advertisements for writing, editorial and publishing services.

Subscription-only magazines include:

◆ *The New Writer*, published every two months. Publishes articles ('creative/literary' rather than hard 'how-to'), several 'opinion' columns, poetry, and short fiction from subscribers only. *The New Writer* now offers its subscribers a regular e-mail newsletter.

◆ *Writers' Bulletin* is a quarterly newsletter carrying news, resources and information for both aspiring and established writers. The *Bulletin*'s editor personally checks out all the information it carries.

◆ *Writers' News*, monthly from the publishers of *Writing Magazine*, carries news, advice, market information, a range of competitions and many ads for writers' services.

◆ *The Author* is the official quarterly magazine of The Society of Authors. Non-members can buy it on subscription.

There are many writers' 'magazines' published on the Internet. Many are freely accessible, and some publish poetry and short stories. (See Chapter 2.)

TIP

Writers' magazines help you feel part of the writing community.

FINDING INSPIRATION AND SUPPORT

Writing can be a lonely business. Some writers prefer to work in isolation, but others need the stimulation of company to spark off ideas and exchange thoughts and views (and complaints about editors and agents). Once you start looking for kindred spirits, you'll be surprised how many you'll find around you.

Writers'circles

There might be a writers' group in your district, or at least close enough for you to attend occasionally. Your library should have contact details.

You can get a *Writers' Circles Handbook*, compiled by Jill Dick, listing contact names and addresses throughout the UK, with regular free updates available after initial purchase. The handbook includes postal workshops, whose members circulate work for mutual comment and criticism. (See page 176.)

The National Association of Writers' Groups is a UK-wide organisation of writers' circles which produces a regular newsletter and holds an annual 3-day conference. Individuals can join as associate members. (See under 'Associations Open to Unpublished Writers'.)

If you want face-to-face contact with other writers but can't find a local group, why not start one yourself? A notice in your local paper (contact the editor) or pinned up in the library should turn up at least a fellow scribe or two. You could meet once or twice a month in each other's homes, or meet occasionally and keep in touch by telephone or e-mail. With enough members, you could hire a room regularly and share the cost.

Meeting other writers in a group can help in several ways. Members provide mutual support, encouragement, and comfort when it's needed, and you can share the cost of subscriptions to writers' magazines and build up a library of writers' manuals and reference books. Members can exchange publications for market study, and club together to buy stationery in bulk.

Your local Arts Council office will advise about inviting guest speakers and will help you to find them. Some Regional Arts Boards have schemes to help groups pay for visiting speakers.

Classes, seminars and residential courses

Most Local Education Authority (LEA) and Workers' Educational Association (WEA) syllabuses include 'Creative Writing' and are advertised in the local press before the start of each term. The library should also have information.

Seminars and courses are held countrywide throughout the year. They're advertised in writing magazines and circulated to writers' groups.

Writers who get involved in seminars and residential courses find that their enjoyment, enthusiasm and stimulation carry over into writing at home and keep them going when they might otherwise become discouraged.

Here are three of the best – see 'Useful Addresses' for contact details:

◆ The Arvon Foundation runs residential courses throughout the year at four centres around the UK, at Totleigh Barton in Devon, Lumb Bank in West Yorkshire, Moniack Mhor in Inverness-shire, and The Hurst near Ludlow in Shropshire. Courses last four-and-a-half days and cover every kind of writing from poetry to novel-writing and journalism, with tutoring by top writers. Grants are available for those who can't afford the full fees. You can get a brochure from the National Administration office.

◆ The Writers' Summer School is held each August at The Hayes
Conference Centre, Swanwick, Derbyshire. The oldest-
established of the British writers' conferences, having run at the
same venue since 1949, Swanwick offers five full days of
concentrated advice on all aspects of writing for publication. On
most days there are two formal lectures by leading figures in the
writing and publishing world – one at 9.30 in the morning, the
other after dinner. As well as the main talks there is a choice of
courses, talks and workshops throughout the week. Send a
business-sized (DL size) stamped self-addressed envelope to the
Secretary. Application forms are sent out in late January.

◆ The Writers' Holiday in Wales, Caerleon is another week-long
writers' 'get-together', organised by Anne Hobbs in late July each
year. Accommodation at Caerleon is in single student-type
bedrooms with *en suite* bathrooms; every effort is made to separate
(noisy) early-risers from (noisy) late-to-bedders – in separate
residential blocks. Food is good. Reservations are accepted up to a
year ahead against a small non-returnable deposit.

Correspondence courses

The value of correspondence courses generates on-going and often
heated debate. One writers' magazine conducted a survey among its
readers and found that success or failure appeared to depend almost
entirely on the calibre of the tutors. The response from course
students, past and current at the time of the survey, also indicated
that the chances of a student being allocated a competent and
helpful tutor are no more than 50–50. Students' comments ranged
from 'my tutor was all I hoped for and more. I have recouped the
cost of the course three times over' through 'kindly comments but
very little constructive criticism' to 'worse than useless – some of the
markets I was advised to send my work to no longer existed.'

It appears, too, that the only qualification needed to be appointed as a tutor is to be a 'published writer' – of what and how long ago doesn't seem to be an issue. Tutors are poorly paid in relation to the cost of the courses, so it seems reasonable to assume that, with a few honourable exceptions, they're unable or unwilling to spend much time on each student assignment. Success would appear to be as much a matter of luck, then, as of hard work on the student's part.

The student drop-out rate is high. According to information from several tutors, many students give up in the early stages, and a significant number do nothing at all after the first or second assignments, even if they've paid the full cost up front.

The bigger schools advertise widely in the national press, in consumer magazines, even on television, as well as in writers' magazines. Smaller enterprises confine their advertising to publications specifically for writers. If you're thinking of signing up, hold off till you get on to the information grapevine, and don't part with your hard-earned before you've seen references. In a 1997 court case, a woman was jailed for six months and ordered to pay back £3,000 in compensation to 53 aspiring writers who responded to her ad for a writing course.

> **WISE WORDS**
>
> Check credentials before you send money to advertisements for courses.

The 'course' was three handwritten paragraphs on finding work as a writer. Think about it: 53 people parted with more than £50 each without making *any* checks.

Your money might be better spent on a selection of writing manuals, or a couple of subscriptions to established writers' magazines, or attending a few seminars or, if you can possibly afford it, a week's residential event.

There are courses available via the Internet, too. It might be worth investigating the longer-established ones.

Writer's block

Before we go on to look at the various types of writing, let's strip the mystique from this much-discussed 'affliction'.

Sometimes called 'frozen brain syndrome', writer's block does exist; illness, bereavement, money troubles, for example, can all paralyse the creative spirit. All too often, though, 'the block' is a self-inflicted problem. You stare at the blank page. You *want* to write. You drink another cup of strong coffee. Still nothing comes. Why?

The reasons are seldom mysterious, muse-dependent or beyond your control. Ask yourself these questions:

Non-fiction

1. Do you care about your subject? Does it move you, excite, annoy, thrill, disturb, infuriate, inspire you? Do you *really* have something to say about it?

2. Or did you choose it because it looked marketable? It didn't look too challenging? You were stuck for ideas? You don't care too much *what* you write as long as you write *something*.

3. Assuming you do have something to say, have you researched the subject thoroughly, and formulated your own ideas about it?

Fiction

1. Do you really *want* to write fiction? Or do you equate 'being a writer' with 'being a fiction-writer'? (Be honest – you won't write anything well if your heart isn't in it.)

2. If fiction *is* your field, have you taken time to think about your characters – what kind of people they are, what has made them that way, what they want, how they're likely to behave, how they'll react to and interact with each other in the situations you plan for them?

3. Have you prepared a convincing background for them, from knowledge and experience and/or research?

4. Have you experimented to find the right storytelling viewpoint and character?

5. Have you allowed time for your story to simmer, to build in your mind till it's boiling over and you can't wait another second to get it down on paper?

In other words, are you trying to write either something that's more of a chore than a pleasure, or something that is not yet ready to be written? In many cases, writer's block results from either lack of involvement or lack of preparation. The cure is in your own hands.

CHECKLIST FOR GETTING STARTED

1. Begin to learn about the writing process and the publishing business. Buy, or borrow from the library, the *latest* editions of *The Writers' & Artists' Yearbook* and *The Writer's Handbook* and read them from cover to cover.

2. If you can't type, take action to learn. Good keyboard skills will allow your brain to focus on *what* you're writing, not *how* you're writing it. If you're interested in writing for magazines and/or newspapers, consider learning shorthand, too; it's essential for

aspiring journalists, and useful, too, for taking notes at interviews and seminars.

3. Join (or initiate) a writers' group. Enquire at the library. Advertise for other writers. Send for the *Writers' Circles Handbook*.

4. Learn about the pleasures and problems you'll have in common with other writers. Subscribe to at least one writers' magazine.

Now you should know:

+ What it takes to become a published writer.
+ What equipment you need.
+ What basic books you need.
+ Where to find information.
+ Where to find inspiration and support.

The Internet

We live in exciting times. Changes we couldn't have imagined even twenty years ago are happening now in our writing world. We have much to gain from the new technology. Don't be afraid of it. Welcome it, use it wisely, and you'll soon wonder how you managed without it. Remember, though, that the Internet is your tool, not your master.

In this chapter:

- what is the Internet?
- what is the World Wide Web?
- using e-mail
- what might the future hold?

WHAT IS THE INTERNET?

Picture a worldwide network of interlinked computers capable of unlimited inter-communication and able both to store and to share information. This vast system is there for us to use, twenty-four hours a day, seven days a week. We can communicate with others and access information all over the world *without moving from our desks*.

There are no borders or boundaries in this electronic world. All you need is a computer, a connecting device called a modem, and a service provider to whom you pay a regular access fee.

You can try out the Internet at many public libraries and 'cyber-cafés' but, believe me, you're going to want your own equipment.

Accessing the Internet

You need to subscribe to an Internet Service Provider (ISP). There are many magazines giving information about ISPs, their services and charges. Check them out before you commit yourself.

TIP

Many ISPs offer free 'no commitment' trial periods and some offer free or very cheap access when you sign up. Be wary of the latter if you're a novice – their help-lines can be *very* expensive. ISPs whose fees include online and telephone help facilities can be more cost-effective.

WHAT IS THE WORLD WIDE WEB?

The two functions of the Internet of most use to writers are the World Wide Web and e-mail (see below).

The World Wide Web (abbreviation www) is a super-huge collection of websites. Each website is a collection of pages linked together under a single domain name, a URL (Unique Reference Locator). Each URL address begins with the protocol http:// usually (though not invariably) followed by www then the specific domain address. Don't be put off by the long strings of letters and symbols that make up web addresses. In practice, the http:// prefix is rapidly becoming a 'given' and is being omitted from printed addresses.

To access a website, you first sign on with your ISP, then call up a search engine, an electronic catalogue. You then key your target URL into the address box, click on a small box alongside it marked 'Search' or 'Go' or 'Find' or something similar. This activates your search engine, which then combs hundreds of millions of pages across the web to find the address you want – in a breathtakingly few seconds.

URLs *must* be keyed in accurately. Even a single wrong letter or symbol will make your request unrecognisable. Life is getting a lot easier, though, as most search engines now let us ask for the address in normal language. (Key in, for example, 'Publishers Catalogues UK' and marvel at the relevant websites listed on your screen.)

The World Wide Web works on the principle of universal readership: *anyone anywhere* can access all the information published there.

DID YOU KNOW?

You can read newspapers published anywhere in the world, with a few clicks of your mouse.

The web opens up a marvellous range of information and resources:

◆ **Research** – You can find information on any and every subject. Bear in mind, though, that anyone, whether individuals or companies, can publish anything they wish, so don't assume that everything you read is accurate and true. Unless you *know* your source is impeccable, double-check everything. Anyone can claim to be an expert on anything – *no one controls the Internet.*

WISE WORDS

Be wary of self-styled experts.

◆ **Markets** – Many magazines now publish online editions, and some show writers' guidelines for their print editions, too. You can also check out publishers' catalogues worldwide.

- **Links** – Nearly every writing website, whatever its topic, offers links to other relevant websites. Links typically appear in underlined blue type. A click on the underlined words calls up the linked website. It's as easy as that. It's also pretty easy to lose track of where you've come from, so if you find a website you particularly like and might want to revisit, you can 'bookmark' the site.

  You can also get involved, if you wish, with online writers' communities and 'chat rooms', where you can 'meet' other writers with similar interests. You could find a writing 'buddy' anywhere in the world.

- **E-zines** – Also called webzines, these are online Small-Press-type magazines that might also be produced in a print version. Most are freely accessible, some ask for a subscription. Some are available to read on-screen, others are sent via e-mail. There are e-zines publishing every topic imaginable, some on subjects so esoteric they couldn't survive in print but can be produced on the web at very little cost, to the delight of their devotees.

  There are also hundreds of e-zines about writing and the writing life, easily found via links in 'writing' websites. To read some e-zines, you'll probably need a facility called Adobe Acrobat Reader, which is free to download from the Adobe website (www.adobe.com).

- **Your own website** – You can set up your own website to promote yourself, displaying examples of your work (as long as you still hold the copyright), your CV and any services you want to offer. Most ISPs offer web-space to set up your own pages as part of the deal.

◆ **Other people's websites** – Many writers with established websites offer other writers the chance to promote themselves, or provide links to their websites, as a mutual deal or possibly for a small fee.

RED LIGHT

Internet sharks will tempt you with offers to display your work on a website, usually at considerable expense, '... so that publishers and agents searching for new talent can read your novel, screenplay, poetry, short stories ...'.

These predators advertise widely in writers' magazines – and their promises sound wonderfully convincing. Don't fall for this. Every agent and publisher's desk groans under work waiting to be read. Manuscripts lie in heaps on their floors. More arrive every working day and there is never enough time to read them all. Where is the logic in claiming that these busy people want to trawl the web for undiscovered talent?

WISE WORDS

One such company used the name of a well known agent in their advertising without permission. Asked to comment on this, at a Society of Authors meeting, this agent dismissed the claim that editors or agents would seek material in this way as 'Absolute b***s**t'.

USING E-MAIL

One of the most useful aspects of the Internet is the facility to send and receive e-mail (electronic mail). It's fast and cheap, and it doesn't intrude at inconvenient times.

Most ISPs allow you up to seven password-controlled e-mail addresses for sending and receiving e-mail. This can be particularly useful for writers who use pen-names.

With e-mail you can:

◆ Write your e-mails offline and have them sent out at a time of
  your choosing.

◆ Keep an electronic address book of contacts.

◆ Send the same message to any number of people at the same time.

◆ Keep copies of all messages sent and received.

◆ Sign up to receive appropriate newsletters, delivered regularly
  (and usually free) to any of your password-controlled addresses.

◆ Send queries to editors (see below).

◆ Deal with corrections and updates quickly and easily.

Sending queries by e-mail

E-mail queries are becoming increasingly popular. In the US, for
example, about 90 per cent of all queries are now sent this way.
Receiving, assessing and replying to queries is faster and therefore
more efficient than by post. This can be particularly useful when
you're working to tight deadlines.

E-mail queries demand different tactics from conventional paper
queries. Here are a few tips to help you get it right:

1. Before you contact any editor, find out if they welcome e-mail
   queries. It's pointless to send out e-mail queries if they're never
   going to be read. Some editors still prefer queries on paper. It's up
   to you to find out the preferred approach. The information you
   need might be in the reference books or on the publication's
   website. If not, check by making a *brief* phone call to the editorial
   department. Check for a special e-mail address for queries.

2. Don't let the technology distract you from the purpose of your query. Your aim is the same as if you were sending a conventional query: to persuade the editor you have a great idea that is just right for their publication and you are the ideal person to write it.

3. Take great care over the wording of your subject line. You need to make sure the purpose of the e-mail is clear and unambiguous. Every e-mail address these days is inundated with 'spam', uninvited e-mails advertising everything from sex aids to get-rich-quick scams. No one reads these, so don't try to be smart or 'intriguing' by writing a teasing subject line – you risk instant deletion, *unread*. Start with the word 'Query', then be brief and to the point. For example, 'Query for your "Current Affairs" section' or 'Query for Mary Smith, Homes Editor' should get your query looked at.

4. Don't be over-familiar or 'chatty'. The ease of e-mail communication tends to encourage informality. Resist this. You won't impress any editor with 'Hi, Mary' or 'Today's your lucky day, Joe'. Word your e-mail query as courteously as you would a letter. Craft it carefully, too, and set it out logically. You want to send a subliminal message that any work they show interest in will be done with integrity and delivered on time.

5. Take care with spelling and punctuation. Don't spoil the impression of care and efficiency with sloppy English or careless punctuation.

6. Don't forget to include *all* your contact information: telephone number, fax number if you have one, and your postal address. Make it as easy as possible for the editor to contact you.

7. Don't overload your query with information. If you have publishing credits relevant to your query, mention these in a brief paragraph at the end. Offer to send samples on request and have photocopies ready to send if they're asked for. *Do not* send attachments with your query. Many editors won't open e-mails

with attachments unless they've been requested from people they know, because they fear their systems might be contaminated by viruses.

8. Don't expect a reply by return. The editor needs time to consider your query. Don't bombard his mail box with follow-up e-mails demanding an answer – he might get fed up with you and hit the delete key.

Recommended reading

The Internet Guide for Writers, by Malcolm Chisholm. Shows how to collect information for your writing and where to find it quickly and easily, so you can save time on research and spend more on writing.

The Internet: A Writer's Guide, by Jane Dorner. Practical, thoughtful, in-depth advice on how the Internet can be of use to you as a writer.

> **WISE WORDS**
>
> Don't send attachments unless and until they're requested.

THE FUTURE

Jason Epstein, former editorial director of Random House and co-founder of the *New York Review of Books*, writes in his memoir *Book Business – Publishing Past Present and Future* (W W Norton, paperback edition 2002) that in his opinion reading on screen may never be the major mode of distribution for books. He believes it highly likely 'that most digital files will be printed and bound on demand at point of sale by machines ... which within minutes will inexpensively make single copies that are indistinguishable from books made in factories.'

Imagine that – pop into a café, select a book from a catalogue on the ATM-like machine in the corner, pay with your debit card, and by the time you've had your cappuccino your book will be ready to collect. Whether you find that prospect exciting or depressing, it could be the future of mass-market books.

The costliest part of the bookselling business is the warehousing and distribution of books. Already many authors are bypassing publishing companies as we know them and publishing their books themselves on the Internet.

Now you should know:

◆ What the Internet and the World Wide Web are, and how they work.
◆ What e-mail is, and how it can help writers.
◆ Some of the current and future advantages for writers.

Understanding
Rights and Contracts

To safeguard your own rights and to ensure that you don't infringe the rights of others, you need a basic working knowledge of how the law protects intellectual property.

In this chapter:

- copyright
- moral rights
- plagiarism
- libel
- rights in book writing
- rights in magazine and newspaper writing
- electronic rights
- co-authorship
- Public Lending Right.

COPYRIGHT

Copyright simply means 'the right to copy'. No one has the right to reproduce, print, publish or sell any part of your writing without your permission. The law protects your copyright during your lifetime and for 70 years after your death. Your copyright is your intellectual property; you can sell it outright if you wish, but you would then have no further claim on that work or on any money made from it.

DID YOU KNOW?

Copyright protects personal letters; the *letter* belongs to the recipient, but the *words* belong to the writer.

In the UK, you don't have to register copyright. It's yours the minute you set your words down on paper.

The copyright line you see in books and magazines – the symbol © followed by the copyright holder's name – warns that the work is protected. You don't have to put this line on your ms – your work is automatically protected.

WISE WORDS

If you're worried about your copyright being infringed, it's easy to protect yourself. Send a copy of your work to yourself by registered post, then deposit the *unopened* package and your dated receipt in a bank. Get a receipt there as well.

If you're tempted to sell your copyright ...

You might be asked to sell your material outright, including the copyright, for a fixed one-off payment. Don't do this, even if the wolf has both front feet inside your door. You might be signing away a fortune.

DID YOU KNOW?

When the von Trapp family fled to America as the Nazis occupied Europe, they sold their copyright for the price of a few weeks' food and lodging. Their story became the multi-million-dollar musical *The Sound of Music*. The Von Trapps never saw a cent of that money.

The copyright laws operate both ways

Just as your work is protected from other writers' plundering, *you* can't quote any substantial part of another writer's work without written permission. And that permission can be expensive. (See *The Writer's Handbook* for current quotation fees.) Permission to use copyright material should be sought from the publishers of that material, and fees can vary from publisher to publisher.

MORAL RIGHTS

The provision of 'moral rights', meaning the rights of 'paternity' and 'integrity', was introduced in the 1988 Copyright, Designs and Patents Act.

The right of paternity is the author's right to be clearly identified as the creator of a work. The right of integrity is the author's right to prevent any distortion or mutilation of his work that would damage his or her reputation.

The 1988 Act requires the author to assert his or her moral rights in writing. You'll see such a notice in the prelims of many books published since 1988.

Moral rights are separate from copyright. The 1988 Act provides for the waiving of moral rights; some magazine and newspaper publishers try to insist that writers waive their moral rights, perhaps implying that such a waiver is a condition of acceptance. Writers are vigorously resisting this. If you're faced with this dilemma, do take legal advice.

'Fair dealing'

This somewhat vague term describes the legitimate use of published material 'for purposes of criticism or review'. This is generally interpreted to mean that you can quote a line or two to illustrate a point you want to make, *provided you give due acknowledgement of the source of the quotation.*

If you want to quote another writer at length, however, or display a substantial quotation in a prominent position in your own work, you would be wise to seek permission. See, for example, page 147, where a page of Steve Wetton's material is reproduced to show how to set out a playscript. I would have no right to do this without Steve's express permission.

Until you're clear about the legal niceties, you would be safer either to avoid quoting from other authors' work altogether or to seek permission for *anything* you want to quote.

PLAGIARISM

Plagiarism is the use without permission of work in which the copyright is held by someone else. You could hit problems if, for example, you were to follow someone else's storyline too closely, or incorporate parts of someone else's work into your own.

> ### DID YOU KNOW?
>
> In 1987, the Estate of Margaret Mitchell brought a complaint of plagiarism against French author Régine Desforges. Mme Desforges's novel trilogy, (published in Britain as *The Blue Bicycle* trilogy), is an obvious re-telling of *Gone With the Wind* in a World War Two setting. The plot and the principal characters have much more than a passing resemblance to those of the famous Civil War novel and Mme Desforges did not deny that the American novel provided the inspiration for her books. She was sued nevertheless, lost her case, and was heavily fined.

You might remember the gaffe made by Princess Michael of Kent when she wrote her book *Crowned in a Far Country*. She included substantial chunks of other authors' works without acknowledgement, and was publicly criticised for this.

Be wary of titles, too. Although there's no copyright on titles, you could have problems if you called your book *Catch 22* or *The Eagle Has Landed*. This could be seen as a deliberate attempt to mislead.

LIBEL

Libel is a statement made in writing or print, or broadcast in any medium, which defames the character of an identifiable living person by holding them up to hatred, ridicule or contempt.

Don't be caught out by an unintentional libel. If you make recognisable use, for instance, of a public figure (or even your neighbour) as the model for a character who commits a criminal act or is portrayed as a 'baddie', you could be sued.

The same caution applies to the use of names. You could find yourself in trouble if you create a villain who holds, for example, a specific position in a company and who bears the same name as a person in a similar company in real life. Check such names with sources like company registers. Take care, too, with company names. If your novel features, for example, a jeweller's shop where someone knowingly acts as a fence for stolen goods, make sure there's no real-life jeweller trading under that name.

RIGHTS IN BOOK WRITING

When a publisher accepts your novel, or commissions your non-fiction book, he will ask you to sign a contract. This document will have many clauses and sub-clauses, and might look dauntingly long and complex. Don't be afraid to ask for clarifications or explanations. It's in your own interest to be clear about what you're signing.

RED LIGHT

Don't sign anything you're not sure you understand.

Contracts vary from publisher to publisher. To show you a specific contract could be misleading or confusing but, basically, this is what a book contract should include:

1. The date of the agreement, the names and addresses of the publisher and the author, and the title of the book – possibly a working title at this stage.

2. The author's obligations.

3. The publisher's obligations.

4. Specification of rights assigned.

5. Provision for revised editions.

6. Specification of royalty.

7. Accounting periods.

8. Warranties and indemnities.

9. Termination and reversion of rights.

10. Miscellaneous sub-clauses pertinent to the particular agreement negotiated.

Subsidiary rights
Scrutinise the small print before you sign. If you've written the kind of book that might attract, for example, film studios or product merchandisers (think *Star Trek*, *Harry Potter*, *Postman Pat*) make sure you're getting a fair deal. Many a fortune has been lost to the author through unwise assignation of rights.

Subsidiary rights include, for example:

- Anthology and quotation rights.
- Condensation rights – magazines and books.

- TV, radio and recorded readings.
- Merchandising.
- Large print editions.
- Electronic rights (see below).

The *offer* of a contract entitles you to approach the Society of Authors for membership. They will vet the document for you *before you sign it*. As agent Carole Blake emphasises in her book *From Pitch to Publication*, your contract is vitally important. It affects every aspect of your writing career.

TIP

If you don't yet have an agent, you might want to approach one *before you sign*. The offer of a contract makes you a lot more attractive as a client, and an agent might be able to negotiate better terms for you.

RIGHTS IN WRITING FOR MAGAZINES AND NEWSPAPERS

Agreements in writing for magazines and newspapers are much shorter and less formal than those for books. Your contract might be no more than a letter stating the terms agreed: wordage, delivery date, payment, and so on.

If the agreement is made by telephone, send the editor a letter recording the conversation, keeping a copy, so there are no doubts about what was agreed. It's important to do this, because by the time your payment is due the editor might have forgotten the conversation, or might even have left. A written record avoids confusion. If the terms are agreed by e-mail, keep printed-out copies.

It isn't strictly necessary to put 'FBSR' (First British Serial Rights) in your covering letter or on your manuscript. The editor will assume that you're offering the right to publish the work for the first time and once only, unless you tell him otherwise. The payment you receive will be a single payment for a single use.

RED LIGHT

When your payment arrives, you might be asked to sign a note on the back of the cheque granting to the publication the copyright in the work they're paying for. This is a try-on. Cross out the note *without signing*. And don't worry – payment will not be stopped, nor will the publication refuse to work with you again.

ELECTRONIC RIGHTS

With the rapid spread of electronic publishing via the Internet, many publishers now include electronic rights in the contract, regardless of their capability or intention to exploit those rights.

You would be wise to hold on to the electronic rights in a work that has future potential as an electronic publication. While few e-publishers are yet making the predicted squillions of dollars, euros or pounds, electronic publishing is a young medium, and the future is unpredictable.

Many rights problems are similar to those of conventional publishing. Although most material published on the Internet can be accessed and read free of any charges beyond your provider's fees, the same restrictions apply to its use, copying or exploitation as to printed material.

The Society of Authors publishes a useful *Quick Guide to Electronic Publishing Contracts*. Like all the society's Quick Guides, it's free to members, and non-members can buy it for £10 post free.

CO-AUTHORSHIP

The law protecting copyright for a specified period after an author's death also covers writing partnerships, such as an artist collaborating with an author to produce an illustrated book, a lyric writer and a composer pooling their talents to write a song, two authors co-writing a book and so on. The work concerned does not come out of copyright and into the public domain – that is, free for anyone to use – until the full period of 70 years from the end of the calendar year in which *the last surviving partner* died.

Don't assume that because one half of a writing team has been dead for the statutory period their work is automatically out of copyright. There was an expensive example of this hazard in the 1960s (when the statutory period of protection was 50 years) involving the partnership of Gilbert and Sullivan, who wrote the Savoy operas. Pye records made a jazz album, 'The Coolest Mikado', based on Sir Arthur Sullivan's music for *The Mikado*. Pye released the record in 1961, but were obliged to withdraw it almost immediately at a huge financial loss. (If you come across one of the copies sold before the ban, it's a collector's item.)

Sullivan had died in 1900, so his 50-years-after-death period was long past. But W. S. Gilbert didn't die till 1911. The jazz arrangements were written and the recording made before Gilbert's copyright ran out, and his copyright protected Sullivan's music. Pye had infringed the joint copyright, and paid dearly for the mistake.

PUBLIC LENDING RIGHT

Public Lending Right (PLR) is a system under which publicly funded payment is made to authors whose books are lent by public libraries. Payment is made once a year, and is proportionate to the number of times a book is borrowed, based on figures from a sample of libraries.

As soon as you have a full-length book of any kind published, register it with the Public Lending Right Office. Ask for a registration form (or download the form from the website). See page 179.

Recommended reading

Helen Shay, *Writers Guide to Copyright and Law.*
Carole Blake, *From Pitch to Publication.*
Michael Legat, *Understanding Publishers' Contracts.*
Society of Authors, *Quick Guide 1: Copyright and Moral Rights.*
Society of Authors, *Quick Guide 8: Publishing Contracts.*
Society of Authors, *Quick Guide 14: Electronic Publishing Contracts.*

Now you should know:

◆ How copyright and moral rights work.
◆ How to avoid plagiarism and libel.
◆ How to handle publishing contracts.
◆ How to handle magazine contracts.
◆ What co-authorship rights mean.
◆ When to register your book for PLR.
◆ Where to find more information.

Keeping Records

Keep simple records of everything relevant to your writing business from the day you start. In particular, keep records of all your financial dealings, so you can submit accurate data to the Inland Revenue at the end of each financial year.

In this chapter:

◆ keeping track of submissions
◆ keeping a markets book
◆ keeping a 'writing only' diary
◆ recording income and expenditure
◆ tax-allowable expenses
◆ handling self-assessment.

KEEPING TRACK OF SUBMISSIONS

Use a record book with pages wide enough to note every submission: when and where you send it, whether it's rejected or accepted, paid for or not and so on. A loose-leaf book works best, so you can add pages as you need them.

Keep a page for each item you write. You need to know what's happening to every article, story or poem.

Item: Short story		*Title*: 'Alien Love'		*Length*: 1,250 words
Date sent	Sent to	Accepted/rejected	Payment received	Date
25.01.200X	*Woman*	Rejected		17.03.200X
03.04.200X	*Dream On*	Accepted	£120	16.09.200X

Figure 1. Example of a submissions book.

KEEPING A MARKETS BOOK

A loose-leaf A4 book gives you plenty of space, and lets you discard out-of-date pages. Record information about individual markets, one market to a page, and note every item you send to that market. For each market note:

1. Information gathered.

2. Every item you send there, with a record of its progress.

3. Your experiences – whether the staff are friendly or offhand, the responses prompt or slow, efficient or not and so on.

4. Changes of personnel, editorial policy and the like.

5. Anything that might be useful for the future (even if it's only 'Never again!').

Dream On 11 Milky Way Starville XX7 7ZZ		Editor: Verity Verruca			
Date sent	Item	Accepted/ rejected	Payment	Date	Remarks
03.04.0X	Short story 'Alien Love'	Accepted	£120	16.09.0X	Slow response but lovely to work with!

Figure 2. Example of a markets book.

KEEPING A 'WRITING ONLY' DIARY

Keep a diary to note, for example:

◆ Deadlines for submissions of commissioned work.

◆ Dates for submitting seasonal/anniversary material.

◆ Closing dates for competition entries.

◆ Writers' circle meetings.

◆ Writers' events you plan to attend.

(Don't forget to cross-reference your writing diary with your social diary.)

You might prefer a set of labelled folders, or some kind of electronic record. Whatever your method, keep it up to date.

RECORDING INCOME AND EXPENDITURE

Any money legitimately spent on your writing business could be tax-deductible against earnings (see below).

By law, you must declare *everything* you earn, however modest, in each financial year. The only exception *at the time of writing* is that competition prizes are not taxable. It's important, therefore, to note every penny you spend – the Inland Revenue doesn't like approximations or guesses.

200X			200X			
June		£ p	June		£	p
1	Black cartridge 41645	24.35	9	'TopTip' +photo		
	Paperclips	0.75		(Gossip)		25.00
	5 reams white A4 paper					
	(John Jotter Ltd)	15.25	21	Article (Snob Gazette)	75.00	
11	Photocopying					
	('Bees' article)	0.25				
14	Book: 'Starting to Write'					
	(Bookbuff Ltd)	14.95				
	Sub renewal					
	(Writers' Bulletin)	20.00				

Figure 3. Two facing pages of a cash book.

If you spend a lot on postage – and most writers do – keep a separate postage book. Enter purchases of stamps and International Reply Coupons (IRCs) in your cash book and log each item posted, with destination, date of posting, stamps used and so on in your postage book. In this way, you'll have to account (to yourself) for every stamp or IRC you use, so you won't be tempted to raid your 'writing' stamps for other letters.

TAX-ALLOWABLE EXPENSES

Get a copy of Inland Revenue booklet *Starting in Business* (IR28), available from any tax office.

Keep all your dealings with the Inland Revenue as open and honest as possible from day one. It doesn't matter how sparse your earnings are, you're required to declare them.

The Inland Revenue allows you to set certain expenses against tax. You need to keep all relevant receipts as well as making detailed contemporaneous notes of expenditure in a diary or record book.

Allowable expenses are those incurred wholly and exclusively for business purposes. The Inland Revenue makes distinctions between 'capital allowances' (equipment like personal computers, fax machines, photocopiers etc.) and 'expenses' (outlay incurred in the day-to-day running of your writing business).

Expenses can include:

- Secretarial: typing, proofreading, researching, indexing, etc.

- Stationery – paper, envelopes, pens and pencils, file cards, even paperclips and staples.

- Postages.

- Telephone calls.

- Internet subscriptions.

- Subscriptions to periodicals relevant to your business.

- Maintenance of equipment used in your business, including computer supplies, software, batteries, etc.

- Travel at home and abroad for meetings with publishers, interviews, research and so on, hotels, car running expenses.

- Photocopying.

- Photography relevant to your business.

- Subscriptions to relevant societies and associations.

- Accountancy and legal charges incurred solely in the course of your writing business.

- TV and video rental, cinema and theatre tickets if solely for the purposes of your writing business.

- Office rental.

- If you work from home, an appropriate proportion of room use, heating, lighting and so on – but do take advice on this, as it could affect your home's exemption from tax liabilities.

Your tax liability is based on your net profit for the accounting year ending in the year of assessment. Take professional advice on the most appropriate date to choose as the end of your tax year. The Society of Authors can recommend reliable accountancy companies experienced in handling authors' affairs.

DID YOU KNOW?

The Inland Revenue have the right to investigate your business for no specific reason, and you would be billed for the cost. You might consider insuring against this. There are special schemes available – take advice from an accountant.

HANDLING SELF-ASSESSMENT

Unless you can afford to employ a professional accountant, you must deal with your tax return yourself. The Inland Revenue do their best to help – take advantage of this. Get a copy of Inland Revenue booklet SA/BK3 *Self-Assessment – a guide to keeping records for the self-employed*. The booklet is available from any tax office, or you can print it off the Internet at www.inlandrevenue.gov.uk/sa/

Recommended reading
The Society of Authors *Quick Guide 4: Income Tax.*
The Writers' & Artists' Yearbook ('Finance' section).

Now you should know:

◆ How to keep track of all your submissions.
◆ How to keep financial records.
◆ Where to find information on self-assessment.

$$5$$

Preparing Your Work for Submission

Your submission says a lot about *you*. When you give an editor a crisp, clean, well set out manuscript, with accurate spelling, grammar and punctuation, you encourage him to have confidence in its content, even before he reads it. You've shown him you care about what you're doing, and that you're approaching the job in a professional way. Even if he turns down *this* offering, you'll have banked some goodwill for the future.

In this chapter:

- preparing a prose manuscript
- dealing with illustrations
- selecting and studying a suitable market
- how agents work.

PREPARING A PROSE MANUSCRIPT

Always follow the accepted standard layout when you're typing short stories, articles or books. (See the relevant chapters for poetry, play-script and picture-script layouts.)

First impressions count

Editors dislike sloppy presentation. Don't imagine they'll toil through a scruffy script, ignoring coffee stains, over-typings, blisters of Tipp-Ex, your bald ribbon or your ink-starved printer, in a tireless quest for literary genius. They won't. They might not read it at all.

You're offering your work for sale in a highly competitive market. Don't turn your customers off with tatty packaging.

Don't rush it. When you've done a complete draft:

+ Check your spelling, grammar, punctuation and syntax.

+ Alter any clumsy phrasing or repetitions.

+ Check that all personal and place names and descriptions are accurate and consistent.

> **TIP**
>
> When you've read each page for sense, read it again line by line *from the bottom up*, covering the lines below as you go. This is a proofreader's trick that throws up faults you can easily miss in a straight reading.

+ Check *any* facts you're not absolutely sure about. If an editor picks up even a tiny factual inaccuracy, he'll worry in case there's a big one somewhere.

+ Finally, check the word count – see below. You should be working with a particular market in mind. Check *now* whether you need to cut any excess wordage.

Calculating your wordage

For an article or short story for a magazine, count every word, and round up to the nearest ten.

Books are different. Look at the text of any novel, for example. While most of the lines occupy the full width of the text area, many do not. Take lines like:

> She looked up.
> 'Oh no,' she sighed.
> 'It's true.'

Here you have just nine words – and they use up three lines.

You'll get a distorted picture if you simply count words. (Computer word counts don't take short lines into account.) Treat every line, however short, as a full line, including the last lines of paragraphs.

This is how to do it:

1. Count the exact number of words in five sets of ten full lines picked at random through the text. Add up these five sets of numbers. Divide the total by 50. This gives the average number of words per line.

2. Add up the total number of lines in your ms, counting every line as a full line. With a reasonably consistent number of lines per page, you can multiply the total number of pages by the average number of lines per page.

3. Multiply the total number of lines by the average number of words per line.

Here's an example:

Total number of words in 50 full lines	=	710
Average number of words per line = 710/50	=	14.2
Total number of pages in the ms	=	193
Average number of lines per page	=	28
Total number of lines in the ms = 193×28	=	5,404
Total number of words = $5,404 \times 14.2$	=	76,736.8

Rounded up to the nearest thousand, your final word count, the figure you would put on your ms, would be 'About 77,000 words'.

Make it beautiful

Present your work like a professional.

♦ Use good quality plain white A4 paper. It will have to stand up to a lot of handling and editorial marking. If you're (still) working on a typewriter, send a good clear photocopy and keep your original for making further copies if they're needed. Never send carbon copies to an editor.

♦ Make sure your ribbon or printer is good enough to produce a clear, sharp, easy-to-read type. Use only *black* ink, and avoid fancy typefaces (Gothic, italic, script and so on). However keen you are to save paper, *never* use a condensed type. Keep the typeface as plain and easy on the eye as possible.

♦ Leave good margins all round, at least an inch, with a bit more on the left to accommodate typesetting instructions. Keep your pages uniform in layout.

♦ Type in double spacing. That means leaving one *full* line of blank space between the lines of type. It *does not mean* leaving a half line of space, and it *does not mean* hitting the space bar twice between words.

♦ To indicate a break in the action, leave an extra line space and start the first line of the next paragraph full out to the left margin, with no indent.

♦ Even if your machine has the facility, don't justify (make even) the right-hand edge. Don't leave extra space between paragraphs, but do indent the first line of each paragraph so that it's clear where the paragraphs begin and end.

♦ Don't underline anything unless you intend it to appear in italics.

Identify your work

Put your name and address on your cover sheet and on the first and last pages of text. Number the pages consecutively, even for a full-length work – *don't* begin again with 'Page 1' at the start of each chapter.

At the top right of each page, type your name, the title (or an abbreviation of it) and the page number. This is called a strap-line; it ensures that your pages don't get out of order (or mislaid).

At the bottom right of every page except the very last, type 'mf' (meaning 'more follows'), indicating more copy to come. Under the last line on the last page, type 'ends'.

Follow the layout as shown in Figure 4.

It really *is* essential to stick to the conventional forms of manuscript layout. These haven't come about by chance, or been chosen at random. They're the layouts publishers and printers have found to be the clearest, quickest, safest and least expensive to work on:

- Clearest because the double-spaced lines of plain black type on white paper are easy to read and less tiring to copy editors' and typesetters' eyes.

- Quickest because the wide margins and double-spaced text leave room for editorial corrections and typesetting instructions to be marked quickly and clearly, and also because they speed length calculations.

- Safest because their clarity reduces the risk of typesetting errors or misunderstandings, even after corrections have been marked.

Short story

700 words

Chriss McCallum

3 The Birches

Rowan Town

Nutwoodshire

ZZ99 7AA

Tel: 0101 01 0110

Make Me an Offer
by Chriss McCallum

The men on the doorstep were strangers. Not that Charley expected to see anyone he knew. He wasn't unsociable. Far from it. He enjoyed company as much as the next man, but he never encouraged visitors.

They were well dressed, smart in dark suits. One was small, thin and neat, ferrety, with eyes as black as boot buttons. A pearl tiepin speared his silk tie. The other man was younger, pug-faced, and a lot bigger. They were friendly and polite, but they didn't fool Charley. He began to close the door, but the big man was already shoving a beefy shoulder into the gap.

Ferret-face smiled and went straight into the old routine.

'... Anything old, anything interesting. Top prices, of course ... old-established firm ... any good pieces ... curios, furniture, quality items ... Hard to find good stock these days. Happy to give you a valuation, sir. No obligation, of course.'

Of course.

Charley thought about telling them to push off, but the heavy shoulder was leaning harder. He wouldn't get rid of them that easily. At his age, physical force was out, and his nearest neighbour was well out of shouting range. And it was getting dark.

He stepped back.

mf

Figure 4. Example of a prose layout.
(Published in *The Writer's Voice* and read on BBC Radio Merseyside)

Ferret-face circled the room, fingers lingering on shabby upholstery, old wood, china figures, lace mats.

'Look, Dennis!' Pale hands clapped in practised delight. 'What a lovely old table!'

'Lovely,' Dennis grunted, cold eyes fixed on Charley.

'Yes indeed, a really nice piece. And this charming sofa – Edwardian, isn't it? Not a lot of call for Edwardian at the moment. Needs re-covering, of course – but it's good. Would you consider ...?'

Might as well play it out, thought Charley. What a charade. He wondered what they were really after.

'Make me an offer,' he said.

'Ah, a practical man, sir, a practical man! I knew it as soon as you opened the door. Let's see now. What do you say to – shall we say, eighty-five for the two items? The sofa and the table?'

'We-ell ...' Charley knew the table and the sofa together would never raise half that amount, the state they were in, let alone cover a dealer's mark-up.

'I can see you've got a business head on your shoulders, sir.' Respect honeyed the reedy voice. 'I'm afraid that has to be my best offer, though.'

Charley said nothing. It'll come out in a minute, he thought.

Button eyes assessed the room.

'Tell you what, sir. We might stretch to, say, the round hundred if you'll throw in another item. What about that old painting on the back wall? No real value there, of course, but the colours are nice and the frame's quite pretty. Might appeal to the ladies. What do you say? A hundred with the picture? You really can't refuse an offer like that, can you now, sir?'

mf

Figure 4. Continued

49

WISE WORDS
Observing professional layouts
will enhance your credibility.

♦ Least expensive because all the foregoing points contribute to speed and accuracy, cutting time-schedules and reducing the need for corrections at proof stage – helping to keep costs down and quality high.

The cover sheet

The cover sheet for the story in Figure 4 would look something like that shown in Figure 5. The layout can be varied, but the important thing is to show all the necessary information.

The final check: Before you pack up your work for posting, give it a final read through. Retype or reprint any corrected pages.

Short story	Chriss McCallum
750 words	3 The Birches
	Rowan Town
	Nutwoodshire
	ZZ99 7AA
	Tel: 0101 01 011
	E-mail: cmcc@nut.net
Make Me an Offer	
by Chriss McCallum	

Figure 5. Example of a cover sheet.

Pen-names

If you want to use a pen-name, type it in the byline under the title, but *not* above your address.

DEALING WITH ILLUSTRATIONS

Good photographs can help sell your work. In fact, some magazines won't consider articles without them.

> **TIP**
> Photographs can double your chances of acceptance.

As soon as you select a market, find out what kind of photos the publication prefers. Some prefer colour transparencies, some like prints, some use a mix, and some use only digital images. With the latter, you need to check for compatibility.

Black and white prints should be glossy, for sharp reproduction. Colour pictures can be either prints, which should be packed between sheets of stiff card, or transparencies, which should be protected by plastic mounts (never glass).

If your submission requires diagrams, maps, line drawings and so on, it's usually acceptable to send roughs for the staff artist to work from, or photocopies if you can supply the artwork yourself.

Don't stick illustrations on to the ms. Pencil *very lightly* an identification number on the back of each one, and pencil the corresponding numbers at appropriate places in the ms margins. Page layouts might not allow illustrations to go exactly where you want them, but they'll be placed as near as possible. Type the captions on a separate sheet and number them to match the illustrations.

SELECTING AND STUDYING A SUITABLE MARKET

For novels and non-fiction books, see the relevant chapters.

If you aim to sell to magazines or newspapers you should have a clear idea of your target market *before* you begin to write your article or story. Too many new writers – and others who should know better – write the piece, revise it, polish it up and prepare the manuscript, *then* start looking for a suitable outlet.

Successful writers don't work that way. They write with a specific market in mind, a market they've already studied in detail. They tailor the content, treatment, style and length of the work to suit that market.

Market study is just common sense

There's no great mystique about it. Think of your writing as a product you're making for sale. No, don't frown and say you couldn't possibly think of creative writing in that way. If you want to sell your work, you *must* think like that. You're taking on a business transaction, little different from selling birdseed or a three-piece suite. You are the manufacturer, and you have to supply what the retailer wants. An editor is a retailer. He buys from the manufacturer – the writer – what he knows he can sell to his customers – his readers.

> **WISE WORDS**
>
> The fiction editor of *Woman's Weekly* won't buy a science fiction story. She knows she would lose readers. Mills & Boon won't buy a political novel. A literary magazine would have no slot for a DIY article. Only the Post Office benefits from misdirected submissions like these.

At the very least, make sure your submission is targeted at the right area of publishing, an area that publishes *that kind of material.*

Start by studying the latest editions of the *Writers' & Artists' Yearbook* and *The Writer's Handbook*. Read right through the appropriate section. Don't just look up the names you know. There might be other potential markets you don't know about.

Select the most appropriate outlets and take a close analytical look to see what prospects they hold for you, as a freelance writer. Send for guidelines if they're offered.

These manuals, however, don't list every possible market. Later in the book you'll find sources of information about markets in the various fields. For the moment, let's look at the general principles of market study.

> **WISE WORDS**
> Shoot with a rifle – not with a shotgun.

1. Check, *before you send anything*, that the market you have in mind will consider unsolicited submissions.

2. Make sure the treatment and style of your work suits your target market.

3. Make sure the length of the work suits the publisher's stated word limits.

Let's look at these points in detail, because if you get any of them wrong you could damage your credibility as well as losing a sale. Careless marketing warns an editor that you're not taking your business seriously.

Are unsolicited mss welcome?
Start with the publication itself. Look at the masthead, the column listing the names of the editor and other staff. There might be a

notice, possibly in tiny print, stating something like 'No responsibility taken for unsolicited mss' (indicating that submissions will at least be read), or 'No unsolicited mss' (meaning that they won't be considered under any circumstances). If there's no information in the masthead, look through the whole publication – it might be tucked away somewhere.

The *Writers' & Artists' Yearbook* and *The Writer's Handbook* can usually guide you on whether unsolicited material is welcome or not. Writers' magazines carry current editorial 'wants' and most check them at source.

If you can't find specific information anywhere, phone (or preferably e-mail) the editorial office and ask.

WISE WORDS

Your market study is your responsibility. It's neither reasonable nor professional to ask another business to subsidise yours.

Don't ask for free sample copies. If it's a trade or professional publication, or one you can't find in the shops, ask if they'll send you a copy or two with an invoice. If they invoice you, pay up.

You can get quicker answers to your questions, of course, if you ring up the editorial office. Most don't mind this, so long as you keep the conversation brief and to the point. Ask for the editorial office at a magazine, or the appropriate department at a publishing house.

Prepare a short list of questions before you phone, so you get *all* the answers you need. You might want to ask, for example:

1. Do you welcome unsolicited material from freelance writers?
2. Are any subjects covered exclusively by your staff?
3. What lengths do you prefer?
4. Do you like a query first, or would you rather see the whole piece?
5. Do you have guidelines I could send for?

Add any other questions pertinent to a particular market. For example, if they answer 'Yes' to Question 1, and you already know what you want to offer, ask for the name of the appropriate editor, so you can address your ms or your query to a specific name.

> **TIP**
>
> Always address your submission to a particular person. This gets your envelope straight on to someone's desk rather than on to an anonymous pile.

Don't go into detail about what you're writing unless they ask you. Be as brief and businesslike as you can. All you need at this stage is basic information.

Is your material suitable?

Submit *only* appropriate material. If you're a beginner, stick to familiar ground and write for publications you already know and like, till you have some experience. You know why *you* buy your favourite publications, you're familiar with their content, so you won't send them something you wouldn't expect to find there yourself.

Get the tone and style right

Collect several *recent* copies of your target magazine. It can be worse than useless to study copies from even a few months ago, because editorial policies change frequently. See Chapter 7 for detailed advice on how to analyse a magazine.

Get the length right

Most of the markets listed in the *Writers' & Artists' Yearbook* specify a minimum and/or maximum number of words. There's no point in ignoring these stipulated wordage limits. Editors have a certain amount of space to fill, and they won't alter either their policy or the size of their product to accommodate a 3,000-word story if their stated limit is 2,000 words. Nor will a 50,000-word novel find a place in a list that only publishes 200,000-word blockbusters.

Keep up to date

You're going into a business that's never static. Magazines vanish, new ones appear. Big publishers eat up little ones. Rebels set up on their own. Editors move about, and take their policies and their favourite writers with them.

Don't rely on last year's reference books. You could waste far more money on misdirected mss than it would cost to update them.

Before you send off *any* submission, then, check that:

- Your target market is willing to consider it.
- What you're sending is suitable for that market.
- You've written the piece in an appropriate style.
- You've complied with the stipulated wordage limits.
- Your market research is bang up to date.

HOW AGENTS WORK

Mention agents at any writers' gathering and you can expect heated argument all round. The most common complaint heard from unpublished or little-published writers is that 'agents don't want to know you till you've already made it'.

This might be true in some cases, but it's far more likely that these disappointed writers' work has been rejected by agents for the same reason most mss are rejected by publishers. Simply, they are not good enough to publish. An agent won't take on the job of trying to

NOTE

Very few agents handle short stories or articles at all except, perhaps, from established book authors already on their lists.

place a book in which he has no confidence, any more than a publisher will accept a book he knows he won't be able to sell.

A good agent chooses his clients very carefully because he'll be committing himself to a lot of work on their behalf. This caution is understandable – the agent makes no money till his author does, and what he eventually makes will be a percentage of what your book earns. Contrary to what some writers believe, most agents work hard for their money.

If an agent does take you on, you'll work together to establish a mutually profitable working partnership. Your agent will secure better terms from publishers, and will know the home *and* overseas markets well enough to exploit the rights in your book as fully as possible. Yes, he gets 10 or 15 per cent of the profits – but *you* get 85 or 90 per cent, and that could well be 85 or 90 per cent of sales you wouldn't have got without the agent.

Try to get an agent if you want to, but be realistic. Your chances of a favourable response are about the same as your chances of acceptance by a publisher. Neither will want a substandard piece of work.

The *Writers' & Artists' Yearbook* and *The Writer's Handbook* both list agents, with information on what they handle and what they don't. Choose one with an interest in the kind of work you're producing, otherwise you'll have no chance at all. Most of the listed agents specify their preferred approach.

Now you should know:

- ◆ How to prepare a prose manuscript.
- ◆ How to deal with illustrations.
- ◆ How to select and study a suitable market.
- ◆ How agents work.

6

Submitting Your Work to the Market

You only get one chance to make a first impression. Make sure it's a good one.

In this chapter:

◆ approaching the market
◆ following up your submission
◆ coping with rejection.

APPROACHING THE MARKET

Every detail of your approach should give a positive impression of your professionalism. Here's how to do that:

1. Whatever you're sending, enclose a covering letter. You want to establish contact with the editor, and your covering letter acts as an introductory handshake. Covering letters and letters of enquiry should be typed as normal business letters, single spaced, *not* double spaced like manuscripts.

2. Keep your letter brief and to the point. You'll find examples in the appropriate chapters. (A letter of enquiry sent by itself, of course, needs more detail.)

3. Find out the name of the appropriate editor. Look in the masthead, check the website, or ring the switchboard and ask for the name you need. *Don't* address anything 'To whom it may concern' or anything like that.

4. Enclose an SAE big enough and bearing adequate postage for the return of your work, otherwise you might never see your ms again. Every publishing office has at least one drawer full of unsolicited mss that can't be returned. The editor didn't invite them, so why should he pay for returning them? Small Press magazines in particular can't afford this expense.

5. If you're sending an ms that's disposable if it isn't wanted, tell the editor so, and enclose a business-size SAE so he can let you know his decision – otherwise you won't know whether you can send it out again or not.

6. If you want to be sure your ms has arrived safely, enclose a stamped self-addressed postcard on which you've written the title of your work and the name of the market you're sending it to.

And how not to ...

1. Don't tell the editor the story of your life, your writing career and how much your family, friends and writers' circle admire your work.

2. Don't embarrass the editor with emotional blackmail. His heart will sink and his hackles will rise if you tell him you need the money to feed your children, or you're 99 and might not survive beyond his next issue, or your doctor has prescribed creative writing as therapy after your breakdown and a rejection could tip you over the edge again. (Yes, people do these things.)

3. Don't be grovelling, condescending or demanding – just be businesslike. Any other approach will cast doubts on your professionalism, and suggest you might be less than a joy to work with.

4. Don't send anything to more than one magazine at a time – editors don't like this. (You *can* send the same proposal to more than one book publisher at the same time. This is accepted practice now.)

5. Don't use umpteen-times recycled envelopes. We all like to save trees – and money – but keep economy labels and sticky tape for your private letters. In business, such economies are counter-productive. They project entirely the wrong image, that of the amateur 'scribbler'. And don't send an SAE that makes the editor cringe and wonder how often it's been licked already. Don't use your day-job company's headed paper, or send your ms in an envelope bearing the company's logo and franked at its expense. This has the taint of petty stinginess, and does not inspire confidence.

Checklist

Before you send anything out, check that:

1. You're contacting an appropriate outlet.

2. You're following the preferred method of approach.

3. You've found the name of the appropriate editor.

4. Your covering letter/letter of enquiry is businesslike and to the point.

5. You've enclosed a suitable SAE with your story or article, or enough return postage with your full-length ms.

6. Your stationery is crisp and clean, as is appropriate to your professionalism.

RED LIGHT

Phrase your letter carefully, weighing the effect your words will have on the editor who reads them. For instance, the following sentences are guaranteed to trigger editorial alarm:

- 'Here is a short story that is a good deal better than those you've been publishing lately ...'
- 'Rejection won't discourage me. It's my life's ambition to get published in your magazine, and I'll keep trying till I do ...'
- 'You will appreciate that I am a beginner, which is why I'm sending my work to you before I try to get published in something more literary ...'
- 'Caution: This story is copyright, and I have taken the precaution of lodging a dated copy with my solicitor ...'

FOLLOWING UP YOUR SUBMISSION

If you don't get a response in, say, four months, enquire about the status of your ms, either by e-mail, letter or telephone. If this gets no response either, you'll have to decide whether to try another outlet or whether you're prepared to wait a bit longer. Most magazines and publishing houses have cut staff to the bone so there's usually a backlog.

WISE WORDS

Always keep a copy of any work you send out.

However, courtesy should work both ways. If you feel you're being dealt with unfairly, advise the editor *in writing* that the ms you sent is no longer on offer. Keep a copy of the letter. (You did keep a copy of the work, didn't you?)

COPING WITH REJECTION

Rejection – a dismal word for a depressing event: an editor has refused your brain-child. It happens to (almost) every writer. Hardly surprising, with dozens of submissions battling for every opening.

The best coping strategy is to build up a regular output. Always have work in hand as well as out on offer. Don't invest all your dreams in one ms.

♦ And if your ms does thud back on to your doormat, *please* don't:

♦ Tear it up and throw it away.

♦ Iron it and send it straight out again.

♦ Write an indignant letter to the editor, questioning his decision, his brains and his ancestry.

♦ Spread jam on the rejection slip and post it back.

Instead, try to analyse what went wrong. Start developing your ability to criticise your work objectively. Answer the questions in the following checklist. Be honest – if you refuse to face the truth you're only fooling yourself.

CHECKLIST

1. Are you sure the work is as good *in every way* as you could possibly make it?

2. Did you check every fact and reference?

3. Are you sure you sent the work to a suitable market?

4. Did you check *for yourself* that your target market is currently open to unsolicited mss?

5. Did you check *for yourself* that the slot you aimed at is not usually or exclusively written by staff or by commissioned writers?

6. Did you analyse your market thoroughly?

7. Did you tailor the style, tone, language and length to your market's requirements?

8. Did you check your spelling, grammar, punctuation and syntax?

9. Did you show an accurate word count?

10. Did you present an ms that is clean, clear, neat, typed on plain white A4 paper, double spaced, on one side of the paper only, with decent margins?

If you answered 'Not sure' or 'No' to any of these questions, your approach has been less than totally professional. It doesn't pay to skimp the hard work.

What if your answers are all 'Yes'? Then perhaps your work was rejected because:

♦ However wonderful you, your best friend or your writers' group believe it to be, the work does not meet publishable standards. Maybe you didn't research, organise or write it well enough – or maybe it's just plain dull. Sorry to be blunt, but these are the reasons for most rejections.

♦ The publisher already has a stock of this kind of material. Yours would have to be sensational to be bought at this time. You're out of luck with your timing – a hazard of freelancing.

♦ The editor has recently bought/commissioned/published something similar. The first two are simple misfortunes. The third could indicate less than thorough market research.

♦ The editor didn't like what you sent him. If he doesn't bother to tell you this, you'll never know. Another editor might love it.

Two questions new writers often ask:

Do editors really read every ms they receive?

The answer to that is 'Yes'. And 'No'. Yes, they look at everything that comes in – no one would consciously risk missing a gem. But no, they don't read every ms all the way through. They don't need to. A rapid scan tells an experienced editor whether a submission is of potential value *to him*. If he doesn't think it is, he won't waste time on it.

It's pointless to try to catch out a 'lazy' or 'prejudiced' editor. So forget the hair or the spot of glue between the pages. They prove nothing.

Why don't editors tell me where I'm going wrong? Rejection slips are no help at all. Why don't they give me the advice I ask for?

Few editors offer advice to writers. Some writers, especially novices, think this is unfair. However, there are good reasons:

♦ Lack of time. With 100-plus mss arriving every week, even a few minutes spent giving advice on each one would occupy hours of an editor's working day – and it isn't his job, anyway.

♦ As explained above, the editor doesn't need to read the whole ms to know if it interests him or not, and advice based on less than a thorough critical reading can be worse than no advice at all.

♦ An editor is employed to fill his publication with suitable material, *not* to give writing tutorials. The writing is *your* job. If you send something that's almost right, the editor *might* give you some pointers and ask for a rewrite 'on spec'. Remember, though, that you're offering work for sale in a commercial marketplace. If you were selling lampshades, you wouldn't ask your customers to show you how to make them, would you?

How books are dealt with

Most publishers employ freelance readers to report on book manuscripts. These are usually experienced editors, authors and academics, and it's on their recommendation that an ms is either rejected outright or passed on to a second reader or an in-house editor.

A publisher's reader has no authority to accept a book, but his decision to reject one is seldom questioned. Acceptance rates for unsolicited book mss are low. One publisher's reader told me he's only seen two out of the 5,000 or so books he's assessed actually get into print. (This is not the glamorous job many people think it is.)

Do keep a sense of proportion, then, if the first publisher on your list rejects your first novel. You're certainly not alone.

DID YOU KNOW?

*M*A*S*H* was rejected by 21 publishers. Enid Blyton collected 500 rejections. Crime writer John Creasey, author of 564 published books, received 774 rejections before selling his first story. Dr Seuss's first children's book was rejected by 27 publishers. John Grisham's first novel, *A Time to Kill*, was rejected by 15 publishers and 30 agents.

If you must let off steam ...

If it makes you feel better, write a nasty letter – but *don't post it*. Such a response would not be forgotten or forgiven.

The following 'rejections of rejections' are not recommended either:

- 'Please read this again. I feel sure you must have missed the whole point of the story ...'

- It was with considerable amazement that I received my returned manuscript this morning. I would have thought that the least you could do was to tell me what you thought was wrong with it. Here is another story. Kindly let me have a swift response, with your reasons in full should you reject this one ...'

- 'How could you! Your rejection has cut me to the quick! I may never have the confidence to write another word ...'

- 'You don't have the guts to give an original talent a chance ...'

- 'I am returning your rejection slip herewith. I regret it is not suited to my requirements at present ...'

Recommended reading

Jack Canfield, Mark Victor Hansen and Bud Gardner (Eds.), *Chicken Soup for the Writer's Soul*.

Barnaby Conrad and Monte Shulz, *Snoopy's Guide to the Writing Life*.

Now you should know:
- How to market your work effectively.
- How to follow up your submission without alienating the editor.
- How to deal positively with rejection.

$$\boxed{7}$$

Writing for
Magazines and Newspapers

Take a look around any major newsagent's shelves. Did you realise that nearly all the publications you see there buy most of their material from freelance writers? Writing factual material for magazines and newspapers offers a fast and potentially lucrative route to publication. The constant demand for good articles makes them the easiest type of writing to sell. However, easy to sell does not mean easy to write. The demand is high, but the standard expected is also high.

In this chapter:

♦ what it takes to write successful articles
♦ finding markets
♦ article types
♦ analysing a magazine
♦ choosing your topic
♦ writing a saleable article
♦ writing seasonal and anniversary material
♦ selling your article
♦ looking at journalism
♦ photography for article writers
♦ writing for overseas magazines

WHAT IT TAKES TO WRITE SUCCESSFUL ARTICLES

Every writer – and that includes you – has knowledge and experience that could interest, help, enrich or simply entertain others. You'll find opportunities in publications about every imaginable subject from architecture to zoology, using writing ranging from readers' letters to in-depth features.

TIP:

A portfolio of published articles will open the door to professional organisations.

To write and sell articles, you need:

◆ The ability to write clear, concise English.
◆ An observant eye.
◆ An enquiring mind.
◆ A professional approach to writing up your material.

FINDING MARKETS

There are literally thousands of potential outlets for articles. *The Writers' & Artists' Yearbook* lists over 600 UK newspapers and magazines that publish (and pay for) articles. *Willing's Press Guide* (expensive – ask at the reference library) lists more than 10,000 UK publications, including trade, professional and specialist magazines. Many of these welcome freelance contributions relevant to their subject areas.

Writers' Bulletin prints in-depth information about editors' current 'wants'. *Writers' News* (and its sister publication *Writing*), *Writers' Forum* and *The New Writer* also carry market news. The Bureau of Freelance Photographers' *Market Newsletter* has market information for photojournalists.

ARTICLE TYPES

Magazines and newspapers use articles of every imaginable type. Look at the choice:

- Readers' letters, fillers and other short pieces.
- Celebrity interviews.
- Personality profiles.
- Personal experience.
- Human interest and 'real life'.
- Anniversary.
- Opinion.
- Historical.
- Descriptive.
- 'How-to' and DIY.
- Self-help and self-improvement.
- Interviews.

ANALYSING A MAGAZINE

To succeed in today's markets, you need to understand your target publication's ethos, style and readership.

General readers look at magazines in a casual way. They notice the cover, glance at the contents list, read the sections that interest them, and maybe flick through the rest. As an aspiring contributor, however, you must take a much closer and more analytical view. You need to build a mental picture of the publication's target readership, to help you understand what the editors and writers are aiming to do.

Get writers' guidelines if they're available, and read them carefully. (Check the reference books, consult the website, or ring the editorial office and ask.) Don't rely on guidelines alone, though. Successful market study needs a 'hands-on' approach.

Take a notepad and analyse your target magazine as follows:

The cover

◆ What does the cover picture tell you about the publication?

◆ What does the text on the cover tell you about the type of reader likely to be attracted to this particular publication?

The list of contents

◆ What subjects are the main features about?

◆ What are the regular 'departments' and columns about? If there's a list of staff names, check these against the bylines – these sections might not be open to freelance contributors.

◆ What kind of articles does the publication appear to favour?

◆ What do the article titles tell you about the writing tone?

The editor's message

Most magazine editors write a comment column in each issue. Read this carefully.

◆ What subjects does the editor talk about?

◆ What do these comments tell you about the magazine's attitude and/or ethos?

◆ What kind of writing style does the editor use?

The readership

◆ Who would the publication appeal to most? Men? Women? Both sexes? A specialist readership? Or a general readership?

◆ In what age group?

◆ What do the advertisements tell you? Advertisers spend their money shrewdly – on ads in the publications most likely to be read by people to whom their products will appeal. Stair lifts and walk-in baths indicate an older age group than sports equipment and family holidays. Catalogue clothing suggests a less affluent readership than department-store fashion. Ads give you a true 'feel' for the readership in terms of age, lifestyle, disposable income, education, interests and hobbies.

The letters to the editor

♦ What do these tell you about the typical reader's attitudes to life: likes and dislikes, interests, social concerns, family concerns and so on?

If there are short stories

♦ What do they tell you about the type of reader the magazine aims to attract?

♦ How many are published in a typical issue?

♦ How does this compare to the number of articles. (See Chapter 8 for detailed advice on writing and marketing short stories.)

The articles

♦ Do they cover a range of topics, or are they narrowly focused?

♦ Are they written in similar styles? Varied styles?

♦ How would you describe the overall tone of the writing?

♦ What kind of leads (introductory paragraphs) do they have?

♦ What type of endings do they have?

♦ Look at the language used: Are the sentences long or short? Simple and straightforward? Or long and complex. Are the words short and everyday? Or multi-syllable and 'Help – where's the dictionary!'?

- Are most of the paragraphs short and sharp? Or long and dense?

- Are photographs included? Sidebars? Graphics? Tables? Other illustrative elements?

- Are the writers named? Are any/most of these names well known? Do any of them appear on the list of the publication's staff?

CHOOSING YOUR TOPIC

If you're a beginner, you could try fillers or readers' letters to start with. A filler is a short item fitted into a small space so that a page won't be left with blank paper where the main items don't quite fill it.

Anecdotes, humorous verse, puzzles, jokes, cartoons, tips and hints, press errors, odd facts, brain-teasers, quotations – all these are used as fillers, and many magazines buy them from freelances.

Keep an eye open for likely filler slots, and collect odd pieces of information, jokes, 'overheards' and suchlike.

Readers' letters have acquired a status of their own and are now a strong selling feature for many publications.

Payment can be as high as £50-plus, but the average is £5 to £10 (more where photographs are used) and some magazines 'pay' in prizes rather than cash.

The 'Letters to the Editor' slot provides a starting point for many new writers. 'Short', though, doesn't equal 'easy'. A successful letter has probably been crafted to its market as carefully as an article.

Points to note:

WISE WORDS

Readers' letters are good practice for an aspiring article-writer because they demand the same kind of disciplines: no waffle, no wordiness, and they must make their point as clearly and concisely as possible.

◆ Are most of the published letters long or short?

◆ Is their general tone neutral? passionate? cosy? argumentative? cynical? amused? helpful? sympathetic?

◆ How many are obvious responses to correspondence or features in previous issues?

Don't bother sending an SAE, unless you're enclosing photographs you want returned. Letters are seldom acknowledged, and no voucher copies are sent. You *might* get advance notice of publication, or you might hear nothing at all till you receive your payment.

Recommended reading
Alison Chisholm: *How to Write Five-Minute Features*, which includes tips on writing Readers' Letters.

When you're ready to move on
The usual advice given to beginners is to write about what you know. That's sound counsel up to a point, but don't let it put you off tackling a subject you feel passionate about. My advice is to write about what interests and inspires you, and to back up your enthusiasm with any necessary research. If you *care about* your subject enough, the reader will know – and your first reader will be an editor.

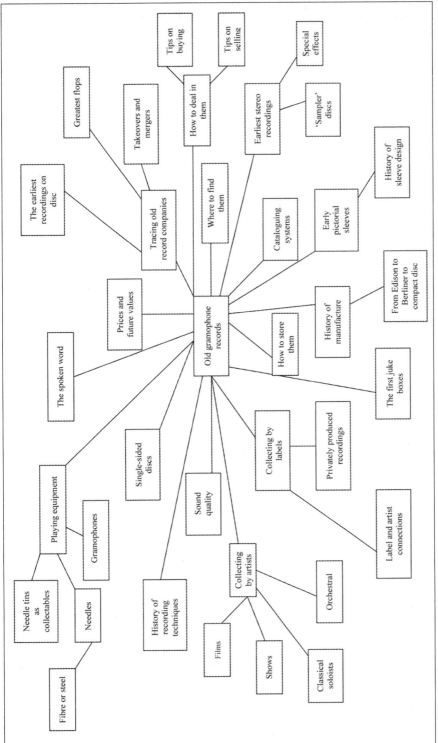

Figure 6. Example of a subject diagram.

Maybe you're already familiar with publications that might welcome your contribution. Could you write more than one article on your subject, slanting each to a different market?

For example, if your hobby is collecting old gramophone records, you could write about:

◆ where to find them
◆ how to store them
◆ how much they cost
◆ the equipment needed to play them
◆ the artists who made them

.... and much, much more, as the subject diagram in Figure 6 shows.

Try making your own subject diagram in the same way. This kind of lateral thinking (sometimes called 'mind-mapping') is far more productive than making linear lists. It's a powerful brain-stormer.

You can also use this exercise to map out information sources, and possible markets. Ideas will come as fast as you can write them down.

WRITING A SALEABLE ARTICLE

Whatever its subject, an article should be structured into a logical and satisfying form. Like a good story, it needs a beginning, a middle and an end, in a straightforward sequence (unlike a story, where you can take liberties with the order of things):

1. A strong opening paragraph. If you've dug up some interesting or little-known fact, or if you have a strong statement to make, put it

here. Beginners often save their juiciest fact till the end. But if you don't grab your reader's interest right away (and remember that your first reader will be an editor, possibly at the end of a long day) he might not bother to read to the end, so your amazing revelation is lost. Feed your reader the tastiest titbit first, and save the second-best to the last.

Example of an opening paragraph:

'For all her success, queen of crime-writers Agatha Christie was a frustrated author. Her world-famous detective creations, Miss Marple and Hercule Poirot, made her rich and famous, but they were "work" and gave her only a fraction of the satisfaction she found in writing her "Mary Westmacott" novels.'

2. The middle section should be packed with interesting information written in the most logical sequence, but not presented simply as a list of facts. Spice it with anecdotes, questions, opinions.

3. The closing paragraph should provide a satisfying rounding-off, summarising in some way what you've been saying. It's a good idea to refer back, however obliquely, to your first paragraph.

Example of a closing paragraph:

'In her autobiography, Agatha Christie described Hercule Poirot as an albatross hanging round her neck. Writers beware – make sure the series character you're working so hard to create is one you love enough to live happily with for years to come.'

Make it convincing

Whatever your subject, it's essential to gather enough information and solid facts to write a convincing, fact-packed article. The editorial nose will soon sniff out a 'scissors-and-paste' job – that is, a piece cobbled together from reference books and other people's opinions. Of course, you can make use of other people's findings and conclusions (provided you don't infringe their copyright), but your article will be stillborn if it isn't enriched by your own thoughts and feelings.

You might find it takes several rewrites to achieve a convincingly 'spontaneous' style, but don't rewrite the life out of it, and don't be afraid to let your own personality show through.

Be methodical

You'll save yourself much time and trouble if you devise a simple system for filing article and filler information as you gather it. It's infuriating if you're stuck for one small piece of information and can't remember where you put it.

You need to be able to retrieve information quickly and easily. This is especially important if your writing time is short, maybe sandwiched between your day job and keeping the weeds down.

You can use document wallets, large envelopes, card index systems, or, of course, electronic storage if you have a computer (don't forget to back everything up). The system itself doesn't matter – what *does* matter is that you have one.

WRITING SEASONAL AND ANNIVERSARY MATERIAL

'Seasonal material' describes writing related to a particular season of the year: Christmas, Mother's Day, Easter, Hallowe'en and so on.

Seasonal material must be submitted well in advance, anything from four months to a year or even more. It's no use submitting a Christmas story in October – the Christmas issue will be ready to print by then.

Check your target publication's seasonal deadlines. Phone the editorial department and ask. No one will mind, provided you're brief and businesslike.

Write your seasonal pieces *during the season*. It's hard to get into a 'mistletoe-and-holly' mood when you're drooping over a hot keyboard on a sweltering summer's day. File the piece away, noting the appropriate submission date in your diary. Get it out a few days early and read it objectively. You might see faults you missed, and this gives you time to correct them and to give the work the final polish that can make the difference between a sale and a rejection.

'Anniversary material' deals with past events, and is intended for publication on or near an anniversary of those events. Like seasonal material, anniversary pieces must be submitted well in advance.

For a beginner, it would probably be pointless to write about an event like D-Day or a Royal birthday, unless you've unearthed something new and/or sensational. You could try a query letter, but most editors will already have material on the subject either in stock or commissioned from regular contributors or from famous 'names'.

Local papers and magazines might welcome features about the anniversaries of interesting local people and events, especially if you can link them to something that's happening today. With local knowledge, you can produce a feature packed with facts and human interest – and that's the kind that sells.

WISE WORDS

Don't refer to current events, unless your piece is intended for that year only. Topical references will make it unsaleable in future years, and stop the magazine holding it on file for the following year.

SELLING YOUR ARTICLE

It's usual now to send a query, either by letter or by e-mail, before you submit an article. This has long been the accepted practice in the US, and most American editors insist on it. Unsolicited material is firmly discouraged.

In the UK, though, it's usually acceptable to send in a very short article. A query letter would take almost as long to read as a short piece of 500 words or so. You won't get a firm acceptance on the strength of a query anyway, so you might as well let the editor see what you can do. If he prefers a query, he'll let you know.

For longer pieces, send a query first. The editor might suggest a different angle, or a shorter or longer length than you suggested.

Writing a query letter

Your query letter should tell the editor:

1. Your subject, and the angle you plan to take. Use bullets to list your points briefly and clearly, and indicate the proposed length.

2. Why you think his readers would be interested in what you have to say.

3. Why you are the right person to write it. If you have special qualifications – practical experience, a degree in the subject, for instance – include them here, but don't drag in irrelevancies. If you're offering an article on Commonwealth commemorative stamps, your 20-year devotion to yoga won't impress.

Suppose you want to offer a general interest magazine an article on collecting ephemera, those throwaway bits of social history: postcards, programmes, tickets, bookmarks and the like. First, check that you have the current editor's name, correctly spelled. Then structure your query something like the letter in Figure 7.

LOOKING AT JOURNALISM

A successful journalist is a writer who knows how to:

◆ tell his story within tightly focused limits
◆ see his story from his reader's angle
◆ avoid verbosity
◆ cut out padding
◆ express his meaning in clear, concise and unambiguous language
◆ produce quality work under pressure, to meet tight deadlines.

Most newspapers, like most magazines, buy material from freelance writers. There are three main types of newspaper: national, regional and local. The *Writers' & Artists' Yearbook* lists all the nationals and a few of the regionals, but *The Writer's Handbook* gives more information in this field, listing all the major national and regional titles, with editorial names and requirements, tips on approaching them, and what they pay.

> **RED LIGHT**
> It's a mistake to rely on reference books for staff names — they could be out of date even before the book is published. Check them yourself.

The financial rewards

Payment varies a great deal. Some papers pay NUJ (National Union of Journalists) rates whether you're a member or not. Others pay 'by arrangement', meaning you'll be offered what the editor thinks the piece is worth – or possibly, if he's never heard of you, what he thinks you'll be prepared to settle for. A thoroughly professional approach can pay off here. Don't encourage the editor to offer you a pittance because your careless presentation and your tatty envelopes tell him you know nothing and care even less about the business.

```
                                        Emily Hoarder
                                        White Elephants
                                        Overflow Lane
                                        Fillingham XX 5 5XX
                                        Tel: 01 001 0001

10 October 200X

David Payer
Editor
Take Anything magazine
Anytown S1 1XX

Dear Mr Payer

Would you be interested in an article about collecting ephemera? There is great
scope in this field for building an interesting and potentially valuable collection,
without too great a financial outlay. Many of your readers might not know how
collectable these scraps of social history have now become. Some might not
know that such a field of collecting exists.

To begin a collection, they would need to know:

◆   what the term 'ephemera' means: essentially items of no intrinsic value, such
    as postcards, cigarette cards, bookmarks, tickets, magazines and
    newspapers, advertising material, pamphlets and so on
◆   where to look for collectable items: antique and collectors' fairs, jumble sales,
    charity shops, the attics and cellars of friends and relations ...
◆   approximate prices they might expect to pay
◆   where the greatest potential lies for increases in value
◆   how to store and/or display their collection.

Once a new collector begins to realise how wide the range is, he or she often
moves on to specialisation, and is soon hooked on the hobby. It's fun, it's fasci-
nating, and it's affordable.

I have been collecting ephemera myself for several years, and have recently be-
gun to specialise in bookmarks, their history and design, and their value to the
companies that issued them (they were widely used as an advertising medium).

The text as I plan it would be 1,750–2,000 words, and I can supply a variety of
photographs, old and new.

I enclose a stamped addressed envelope, and look forward to hearing from you.

Yours sincerely

Emily Hoarder.
```

Figure 7. Writing a query letter.

Unless you're already a member of the NUJ, there's no point in challenging the offer. Either refuse it and try your luck elsewhere, or accept it philosophically so you can add another item to your tally of published work. A strong portfolio will eventually put you in a position to negotiate fees, as more and more publications are asking for clips to be included with proposals.

> **TIP**
> Each edition of *The Writer's Handbook* gives current NUJ payment rates for national and provincial newspapers and for magazines.

Getting your foot in the door

You could try local papers. They always want:

♦ News stories, short and to the point, covering local events: 'Her Majesty unveils memorial plaque', 'local grandmother's surprise triplets'.

> **TIP**
> 'Local' means keeping the focus on the area. For example, 'Main Street grocer lost at sea' could refer to someone lost with the *Titanic*.

♦ Social issue articles: 'Save our swimming baths!', 'Do our citizens want clean streets?'

♦ Striking photographs of local people, places and events.

If you spot an opening for a topic your paper isn't already covering, you could suggest ideas, perhaps for:

♦ A book, film, TV or DVD column.
♦ A poetry corner.
♦ A children's page.
♦ An original series that *you* could supply on a regular basis.

But don't suggest any kind of competition unless you're willing to handle the entries yourself. The staff won't welcome the extra work.

The five 'W's

When you're writing your article, make sure you include all essential information. Check the content against the journalist's creed, the five 'W's:

- Who?
- What?
- Where?
- When?
- Why?

And if it's appropriate, add an 'H' for 'How'?

Whether distributed free or not, these papers live on their advertising revenue, so short pieces stand a better chance because they leave more room for ads.

Include a photograph or two if you can. Check with the paper about preferred formats.

Check deadlines, too – this week's hot news is next week's rejection.

You'll usually be paid after publication, at some set date, and you might be expected to submit an invoice. Clarify this beforehand. An invoice is a simple business document, a bill asking for payment of money due to you. It's easy to prepare. Just make sure you include all the necessary information, as in Figure 8.

```
                              INVOICE
                                           Oliver Columnist
                                           12 Gossip Alley
                                           Tiny Tiles
                                           Eastborough X12 21X


22 July 200X

Basil Bond
Editor
Eastborough Times
Eastborough A22 22X

To supplying one short feature: 'Scandal at the Vicarage'
Plus 3 b/w photographs
Published in Eastborough Tattle 15.7.0X          £35.00
```

Figure 8. Example of an invoice.

PHOTOGRAPHY FOR ARTICLE WRITERS

You'll increase your chances of success many times over if you can supply the right kind of photographs to supplement your articles.

When you're researching your market, note what proportion of photographs to text your target publication uses, what proportion of colour to black-and-white, then check with the editor:

- whether they use photos supplied by the writer – some publications prefer to use staff photographers or library photos

- if they do want your photos, what format they prefer

- how they like the photos to be supplied.

> **TIP**
> Not all publications accept digital photography, so check before you invest in a digital camera.

Consider subscribing to the Bureau of Freelance Photographers, where you can get technical advice and market information specially gathered for photographers and photo-journalists. (See under Associations Open to Unpublished Writers.)

Recommended reading
Jill Dick, *Writing for Magazines.*
Chriss McCallum and Gordon Wells, *The Magazine Writer's Handbook*, 9th edition.

WRITING FOR OVERSEAS MAGAZINES
The whole English-speaking world is open to you, and it's huge.

The Writers' and Artists' Yearbook lists a selection of overseas book publishers plus details of magazines and newspapers in Australia, Canada, New Zealand, and South Africa. For the USA, the *Yearbook* gives information on book publishers and literary agents in various countries overseas, but doesn't list specific magazines or newspapers, referring readers to other sources of information.

The Writer's Handbook has substantial sections on US book publishers and literary agents, plus US contacts based in the UK.

The Internet has more information than you could ever use on overseas magazines, newspapers and book publishers. Ask your favourite search engine to find, for example, 'magazines North America' and you'll see lists that would take weeks to explore. Choose your country and take your pick. Most magazines post guidelines on their websites, and many let you read current or past issues on-screen.

Rights

You can offer material already published in the UK to overseas magazines *provided you've only sold British rights.*

Although both publications cover copyright law, neither the *Writer's & Artists' Yearbook* nor *The Writer's Handbook* give guidance on rights bought by specific magazines. *Writer's Market,* on the other hand does give this information for magazine submissions.

Writing for North American markets

The most comprehensive guide to North American markets is *Writer's Market,* published annually by Writer's Digest Books, Cincinnati. With more than 1,000-plus pages in every edition, *Writer's Market* is packed with markets for every kind of writing, with details of pay rates, royalties, advances, specific editorial needs and submission guidelines. You can order it through major bookshops, or find the online version at www.writersmarket.com

Nearly all US magazines issue comprehensive writers' guidelines. They find this saves time and trouble for their staff as well as for potential contributors. With Internet access, you can look them up on the websites. Alternatively, you can request guidelines by post from most print magazines. Send a self-addressed envelope (C5 size is usually big enough) plus two IRCs.

Invest in an American-English dictionary. The quip that the US and the UK are 'divided by a common language' is not a myth – many spellings are different, as are some meanings, so don't risk getting caught out using a word or phrase that might not mean what you think it does. You can find some American magazines and newspapers on our newsstands. Read them – you need to familiarise yourself with current usage.

Since the attacks of 11th September 2001 American publishers are wary of any package from an unknown or unexpected source. You need to make an initial enquiry by e-mail or even by telephone. When you follow up your query, address your package clearly to the particular editor who agreed to look at it, and mark it 'Requested submission'. *Do not send any kind of package without taking this precaution.*

Markets worldwide

With access to the Internet, you can find information about English-language markets all over the world. For example, key in 'English language magazines'. In seconds you'll have leads to English language magazines worldwide.

You can read the magazines online, see their guidelines, send article queries and book proposals by e-mail ... (Are you *still* wondering if it's worth getting a computer?)

The 'ex-pat' market

Don't overlook the magazines specifically produced for British people living abroad. Look at www.expatriates.com to see the range of markets open to English language contributions. Whatever your interests, you'll find at least one or two potential outlets.

Now you should know:

- What it takes to write successful articles.
- How to find markets.
- The various article types.
- How to analyse your target publication.
- How to write a saleable article.
- How to sell your work.
- Where to find information about overseas markets.

8

Short Stories

For an earlier edition of this book, we asked readers to complete a questionnaire about their writing interests. We were not surprised to find that short-story writing was favourite. What *did* surprise us was the extent of the short story's lead. It stood 20 percentage points above its nearest rival, the novel. It isn't hard, then, to see why the competition to get short stories published is so fierce.

In this chapter:

- stories that sell
- choosing a market
- analysing your market
- stories for the Small Press
- how to be your own editor.

Other than two or three magazines aimed at women readers, short story publications don't sell well – even to writers who want to get published there. Short story collections sell poorly, too. Yet the competition to get short stories published is as keen as ever. To succeed, then, you need more than talent and luck.

Don't be put off, though, by writers who complain that 'You can't sell short stories these days – editors don't want them....' Complaints like this invariably come from unsuccessful writers who don't – or won't – recognise the true situation: magazines that use short stories can't get enough of the well written, entertaining, satisfying short stories their readers want.

STORIES THAT SELL

Every day, editorial desks sag under piles of dull clichéd sermonising stories, lifeless formless pointless stories, sad sordid despairing stories ... Editors don't want them. Their readers don't want them.

A good short story needs:

- A single storyline, without sub-plots.
- Three or four characters at most.
- A single viewpoint, or two at most.
- A short time-scale.
- Consistent mood, tone and pace.
- Consistent writing style.
- Appropriate language.
- Brief descriptions.
- Minimum background.
- Concise dialogue.
- No lengthy preamble.
- No contrived ending.
- No preachy message.

WISE WORDS

You *can* learn how to do it. Read books on the craft. Read, study and analyse published short stories by today's successful writers.

CHOOSING A MARKET

We'll look at a few here, to give you a start. Then you must dig them out for yourself, from your newsagent's shelves, writers' magazines, the *Writers' & Artists' Yearbook* and *The Writer's Handbook*. Look out for new publications appearing on the newsstands. Read the *Press Gazette* to keep up with new launches.

Look beyond the obvious outlets. Search among specialist and hobby publications – some of these will consider short fiction relevant to their subject. Some regional magazines and newspapers publish short stories, too.

Women's magazines

This is the biggest paying market for short stories. You don't have to be a woman to write for them. You don't even have to write 'women's' stories. Some editors prefer male writers to adopt a feminine pen-name, but masculine bylines appear more often these days.

Publishers D C Thomson & Co are very helpful to promising new writers. They're always keen to find writers who can supply the right kind of fiction for their publications, which include *My Weekly* and *People's Friend*. They also need serial stories for the weekly magazines, and short romantic or romantic-suspense novels, 35–40,000 words long, for My Weekly Story Library.

The fiction editor of D C Thomson offers this advice: 'D C Thomson are always in the market to find good new writers for their wide range of publications, as shown by the many different leaflets we provide.

'New writers have to face the fact that competition for success is fierce. Because of the volume of contributions received, encouragement of new writers can only go to those who show most promise in producing our kind of material.

'Once you have studied the market, send your story to the editor of the magazine at which it is aimed or to the Central Fiction Department which acts as a clearing-house for unsolicited contributions.'

Note the phrases: 'our kind of material' and 'once you have studied the market'. You have to show not only better than average writing ability, but also an awareness of the company's needs. They offer encouragement and advice, *not* tuition in writing. D C Thomson will supply their guideline leaflets on request – send a large SAE. The leaflets include writing for their women's magazines, for My Weekly Story Library, for children's and teenage picture- and photo-story scripts, and give details of how to submit your work.

ANALYSING YOUR MARKET

Get guidelines if you can. They'll give you a magazine's basic requirements. You'll increase your chances considerably, though, if you build up your own detailed study.

Collect *at least* six issues of your target magazine – a glance through one or two copies is not enough. Read again the advice in Chapter 7 on 'How to analyse a magazine'. You need a clear picture of the magazine's readership and its overall tone and style.

Now concentrate on the short stories:

◆ How many words? The guidelines could specify '750 to 2,500 words', but you might find that most stories are between 1,000 and 1,500 words, with only one or two as short as 750 words or as long as 2,500 words. You could have a better chance with stories in the more favoured lengths.

◆ What viewpoint do the stories use? First person? Third person? More than one? If *all* the stories in your sample issues are written in first person, don't waste your time sending a third-person viewpoint story. A mix of viewpoints might suggest that the editor has no strong preferences, but it's worth assessing which viewpoint is used most.

◆ What kind of stories appear most often? Romantic? Mysterious? Suspenseful? 'Twist-in-the-tail'? Spooky? Other?

◆ How many main characters per story?

◆ How many stories have a female main character? How many favour a male?

◆ What age group are most of the characters in?

◆ Do the characters have anything in common? Are they mostly single? Married? Widowed? Divorced?

◆ What kind of names do they have? 'Everyday'? Or 'posh'?

◆ What kind of occupations do they have? Housewives? Shopworkers? Secretaries? Teachers? Media-workers? Models? Self-employed? High-flyers?

◆ What kind of relationships feature most often? Harmonic? Difficult? Stable? Shaky? New? Settled?

◆ What kind of backgrounds appear to be favoured?

◆ Do most stories feature love scenes? How explicit are these?

◆ How do most stories begin? With descriptive narrative? With dialogue? With action?

◆ How do most stories end? Happily? Loose ends tied up? Hopeful? Satisfactory? Teasing? Leaving readers to draw their own conclusions?

WISE WORDS

Keep your writing style simple and straightforward. Avoid any kind of contrived style or language that might intrude between your reader and what you want to tell him. Write to express, not to impress.

Every editor lives in hope of finding a wonderful story in the morning post. The more you know about your target publication, the better your chances of making an editor's day.

STORIES FOR THE SMALL PRESS

The Small Press plays a significant part in nurturing our country's writing talent. Who else will welcome our quirky, off-the-wall short stories, our experimental poetry? Who else will publish cutting-edge writers without fear of alienating shareholders, corporate boardrooms, or big-money advertisers? Small Press editors publish what they like – and what they like is original, innovative prose and poetry, the kind that might not be welcomed in the high-powered commercialism of the world's IPCs and EMAPs.

There's a downside to independence, of course: the problem of funding. A few magazines receive Arts Council grants, some are stocked by larger bookshops, but most survive entirely on subscriptions. They're nearly always produced on a minimal budget by a single enthusiast or a small team working in their spare time and relying on reciprocal advertising for publicity.

Every editor I know gives the same advice: 'Read the magazine you want to write for.' There is never a shortage of writers wanting to contribute material. Competition is tough, so you need to know what the editor likes.

Small Press magazines can do a lot for writers, especially those who have yet to find their niche or make their mark in the literary world. Many have status beyond the Small Press world, and quite a few writers who got their start there continue to support them and to contribute work.

Independent magazines receive far more submissions than they could possibly use, yet only the most successful can afford more than a token payment, and many can give only complimentary copies. Writers themselves

DID YOU KNOW?
William Boyd, Graham Swift and Ben Okri all had early works published in the Small Press.

could do much to improve this situation. The arithmetic is simple: if every writer who wants to be published in the Small Press actually *bought* a magazine, there would be hundreds more markets able to pay what good writing deserves. Wouldn't we all benefit from that?

Study these markets, too

Always study *at least* one issue of a magazine before you submit any work. You need to digest its style and flavour. Not every magazine will suit you, of course, so search out those that do.

You don't have to commit yourself to a subscription – most magazines will sell you a single copy on request. But please *don't* ask or expect them to hand out free samples. These small businesses struggle to survive – they can't afford to subsidise your market study. Remember, too, *always* to enclose an SAE with every submission or query.

Light's List offers a huge choice of Small Press magazines worldwide. See page 176.

HOW TO BE YOUR OWN EDITOR

Do revise and rewrite – objective self-criticism is a skill worth practising. These are some of the faults and weaknesses that might cause your story to be rejected:

1. Is the opening too long? Too slow? Too general? It's vital to grab the reader from the opening paragraph.

2. Have you begun in the right place, at an intriguing point in the action? Avoid the leisurely preamble – get right into the story.

3. Have you used flashback? Too much 'history' can kill your story's pace.

4. Have you developed your characters and portrayed them through their actions, reactions and interactions rather than by bald exposition?

5. Have you sustained momentum throughout, moving the story on through cause and effect? Or have you cluttered the narrative with unnecessary detail and superfluous characters? Your hero might be reminded of his good fortune when he sees a beggar, but we don't need to know how Betty the Baglady fell on hard times. Keep the focus where it belongs.

6. Is the ending satisfying, believable, and logical in the story's own terms? Or did you run out of steam, leave loose ends, or introduce a contrived 'twist' or a new character who provides all the answers?

7. Is the viewpoint consistent? The tiniest shift can destroy the reader's empathy. For example, your hero sees his lost love: 'David felt his heart thump, and tears began to sting his blue eyes ...' The single word 'blue' is an observation *from the outside*, requiring us to look *at* David rather than feel *with* him.

8. Have you given your characters suitable names? Take care not to 'place' your characters in inappropriate age bands or social categories: 'Ada and Herbert', 'Tracey and Kev', 'Camilla and Peregrine' – names like these evoke different perceptions and expectations.

9. Is the dialogue natural? Or does it seem stilted and unconvincing? Read it aloud, tape it if possible, and listen for awkward phrases and out-of-character speech patterns and vocabulary. Use abbreviations: 'couldn't', 'he'd', 'they'll' and so on – where they feel right.

10. Have you left the reader space to use his imagination - or have you described every move, thought and feeling? We don't need to know every detail of every scene. Don't be afraid of 'jumps' in time and place. This will lend pace to your story, too.

11. Is your spelling sound? Careless spelling can alter or fog your meaning, and gives the editor negative messages about you.

12. And your punctuation? Careless punctuation can produce nonsense: 'The rain was pouring down Carol' does not mean the same as 'The rain was pouring down, Carol'.

13. And your syntax? Syntax is the ordering of words to convey a clear and unambiguous meaning. Try this: 'The mayor arrived to light the bonfire with his wife.' The right words are there, but their order makes the statement absurd. Make sure you've said what you meant to say.

14. Are your tenses consistent? It's all too easy to shift from present to past and vice versa without noticing.

15. Is your writing concise and sharp? Or wordy and slack? Tight writing has more impact. Especially, avoid weak verbs that need supporting adverbs: a branch *fell heavily* to the ground – try *thudded.*

16. Have you used *active* rather than *passive* verbs? 'Fido chased Felix' is stronger than 'Felix was chased by Fido'.

17. Have you avoided vagueness? 'A crowd was waiting to see the parade' is woolly. 'Crowds waited ten-deep along the parade route' is more vivid.

18. Is your text repetitive? Don't bore your reader with 'Mary's mother said this' and 'Mary's mother said that', 'Suddenly this' and 'Suddenly that'. Vary your vocabulary.

Recommended reading

Iain Pattison, *Cracking the Short Story Market.*
Stella Whitelaw, *How to Write Short-Short Stories.*

Now you should know:

◆ What makes a saleable short story.
◆ How to choose and analyse a market.
◆ What opportunities the Small Press offers.
◆ How to criticise and edit your own work.

9

Your First Novel

To bring a novel from inception to publication can take two or three years. Publishers have to think ahead. So does the smart writer. Don't waste your time trying to cash in on today's hits. Write the novel you're burning to write, and make it as good as you possibly can. There is only one rule: don't bore your reader.

In this chapter:

◆ getting to know the book business
◆ the different types of novel
◆ checking your manuscript for fatal flaws
◆ preparing your submission package
◆ marketing your novel.

GETTING TO KNOW THE BOOK BUSINESS

Read the weekly trade 'bible', *The Bookseller*. Subscriptions are not cheap, although they include the special spring and autumn 'Buyers' Guide' issues and give you subscriber access to the *Bookseller* website. If you've made a friend of your local bookseller (and you should) he might let you browse through his copies.

Read the 'Books' pages in the Sunday broadsheets, too. They often include current book trade information and news (and the odd bit of gossip).

THE DIFFERENT TYPES OF NOVEL

In most writers' manuals, you'll see references to 'general' or 'mainstream' and 'genre' or 'category' fiction. Publishers 'label' novels for ease of reference.

Every issue of *The Bookseller* lists 'Publications of the Week'; these are categorised lists of all the books published that week. The 'Fiction' category is divided thus:

- General – a huge variety that includes 'literary' fiction.
- Action-adventure.
- Historical.
- Mystery, which includes 'crime'.
- Romance.
- Science fiction, which includes 'fantasy' and 'horror'.
- Short stories – collections from individual authors and anthologies, in book form.
- Thrillers.
- War.
- Westerns.

These listings include any and every combination of the above types – you could write sci-fi Westerns, romantic thrillers, historical action-adventure ... Don't let any thoughts of 'fitting into a category' stifle your imagination. Go with whatever inspires you.

Complete your novel before you try to sell it
If you've never written a novel before, you would be wise to complete your manuscript *before* you approach the market. In today's fast-moving publishing world, few editors and agents are willing to work with a new author on the basis of an outline and sample. You have to be able to show you can deliver what you promise.

Writing a whole novel takes a lot of stamina and probably a lot more time than you think. You want to be in a position to respond quickly if an agent or editor likes your submission package and asks you to send the whole novel. If you've still got months of work to do on it, you might lose your chance.

CHECKING YOUR MANUSCRIPT FOR FATAL FLAWS

Put your manuscript away for at least a couple of weeks, then read it right through, asking:

1. Have you kept the spotlight on your basic theme and main characters? Sub-plots and minor characters should not overshadow these.

2. Have you developed your characters fully, portraying them through their actions, reactions and interactions, and keeping them 'in character' throughout? Don't let them act out of character without a good reason.

3. Has your protagonist changed (or been changed) by the end? A main character who neither changes nor grows in some meaningful way between the first and last pages will be static and unconvincing.

4. Is your story logical? Even a fantasy needs to make sense within its own terms.

5. Does the story maintain a satisfactory 'cause and effect' sequence, with each event following on logically from what has gone before? A plot that relies on coincidence, for example, or the convenient arrival of a new character, will strain your reader's credulity. Coincidences do happen in real life, but they're seldom convincing in fiction.

> **WISE WORDS**
>
> Avoid coincidences in your plot – they'll strain your reader's credulity and make him feel cheated.

6. Have you kept control of your chosen narrative voice (or voices) throughout? Check for unintentional switches or slips of viewpoint?

7. Does every scene take the action forward, enrich characterisation, increase tension, or provide a calming or reflective interlude? If it does none of these, ask yourself why it's there. Could it be cut without harming the story?

8. Check every piece of dialogue – is it 'in character'? Does it contribute to characterisation and/or move the story forward?

9. Have you been sparing with description and explanation, leaving room for your reader's imagination to come into play?

10. Is the writing strong, evoking all the senses? Have you used passive voice where active voice would work better? Have you used 'to be' verbs supported by adverbs where strong verbs alone would be more effective? Flabby writing can dull the impact of the most brilliant story.

11. Look again at the story as a whole. Is the structure balanced? Have you begun in the right place? Don't jeopardise your chances by starting the story too early, providing too much background and taking too long to get things moving. Many a story has been saved by cutting out the first chapter and plunging straight into the action.

12. Have you sustained momentum through the middle section, moving the story on through cause and effect, action and reaction, tightening tension as you build to the climax?

13. Have you left your reader feeling satisfied that the whole story has been told? Make sure you haven't left any unintentional loose ends.

14. Are you absolutely sure your novel is as good as you can make it?

PREPARING YOUR SUBMISSION PACKAGE

Whether you intend to send your work to an agent or straight to a publisher, you need to prepare a submission package. An agent or editor must be able to assess your novel quickly and easily. *Never send your complete ms until you're asked to do so.* Your package should consist of:

◆ A covering letter addressed to the agent or editor *by name*. Show them you selected them with care and not by sticking a pin in the *Writers' & Artists' Yearbook*. Don't offer either your own or anyone else's opinion of the story. Only the agent or editor's opinion matters. (See Figures 9 and 10.)

Dear Hope Hitfinder

I write to ask if you would be interested in representing my mystery novel 'Did He Fall?', complete at 90 thousand words. A second novel featuring the same main characters is already in outline, and I have ideas for further titles.

I am approaching you because you represent several authors, including 'X, Y and Z', whose work I admire.

Mystery and crime novels have always been my favourite reading, and I believe 'Did He Fall?' would fit well into the 'mystery' genre.

I enclose a brief blurb, biographies of the four main characters, a synopsis, the first two chapters, and my author biography.

Sincerely,

Millie Author

Figure 9. Example of a covering letter for a novel submission to an agent.

Dear Barry Editor

I write to ask if you will consider my mystery novel 'Did He Fall?' for publication. The novel is complete at 90 thousand words. A second novel featuring the same main characters is already in outline, and I have ideas for further titles.

I am approaching you because you have published several books I've enjoyed, particularly 'A' by 'B' and 'X' by 'Z'. I believe 'Did He Fall?' could suit your list.

I enclose a brief blurb, biographies of the four main characters, a synopsis, the first two chapters, and my author biography.

Sincerely,

Millie Author

Figure 10. Example of a covering letter for a novel submission to a publisher.

- A *brief* blurb, no more than one or two paragraphs. The blurb is intended to *sell* the story, in the same way as the blurb on the cover of a published novel sells it to the prospective reader. (See Figure 11.)

- Brief biographies of your most important characters, no more than one or two short paragraphs for each character. Think these out carefully – it's essential to show that your characters have the potential to make readers care about them. (See Figure 12.)

- A concise synopsis of the whole novel, written in the present tense. Touch on key scenes, making clear who is your main character, what their ultimate goal is, who and what stands between them and that goal. Show how the story ends. New writers often try to conceal the ending in an attempt to intrigue.

'Did He Fall? blurb:

Former police detective-inspector Jake McKinlay believes he has left his bad times behind. He has moved to the city where his ex-wife and young daughter now live, and has made peace with them. Unwittingly, he puts his hopes of a possible reconciliation at risk when he agrees to help his ex-wife's friend Laura Canning investigate the death of her uncle, impresario Max Laurence. Laura believes Max did not drown by accident, and that there has been a cover-up.

Jake finds himself attracted to Laura and, through her, he is drawn into the strange world of Max's family, where undercurrents of tension grow as he uncovers long-hidden secrets someone in the family is desperate to keep concealed. The deeper he probes the more dangerous the secrets he uncovers, until he finds himself, Laura, and his own child in mortal peril.

Figure 11. Example of a 'selling' blurb.

'Did He Fall?' main character biographies:

Jake McKinlay, 42, just under six feet tall, physically slim and strong, but walks with a slight limp, legacy of the incident that got him prematurely 'retired' from the police force. Always a maverick, he drank too much and sometimes strayed across the line of legality in his investigations. Doesn't drink now, but stays sober the hard way, without any support network.

Loves blues music and Western films. Divorced but renting a flat from his wife above the pet store she owns. Still cares for his wife and adores his eight-year-old daughter Amy. Now making the first moves towards setting up as a private investigator.

Laura Canning, 35, mother of a ten-year-old daughter. Medium height, slim, dark-haired. Professional photo-journalist specialising in theatre. Living apart from her husband, having moved back to her family home to consider her future. The failure of her marriage has severely dented her self-confidence and she is afraid to trust her own judgement about Max's death.

Figure 12. Examples of character biographies.

This is a big mistake. The agent or editor needs to be able to assess the story as a whole. (See Figure 13.)

'Did He Fall?' synopsis:

As he begins to settle into his new home in the historic city of York, life is looking up for Jake McKinlay. At last he feels he is getting his life into some kind of order following years of fighting his drinking habit while scraping a living any way he could after getting compulsorily if discreetly 'retired' from his job as a detective inspector in Glasgow CID.

Today, he has thrown the windows open to the spring sunshine and is starting to hang his treasured collection of Western film posters, feeling at last that it's worth making the small flat look as if he might be staying for a while.

He is pleased when his ex-wife, Sally, rings him from the pet shop she runs on the ground floor of the building. He is trying very hard to repair some of the damage he has caused in their lives. Sally brings her friend Laura Canning up to his flat, where he is brewing a pot of coffee to welcome them. Sally asks Jake a favour on Laura's behalf. Will Jake use his experience as a detective to look into what Laura maintains is the suspicious death of her uncle, Max Laurence.

Jake agrees, mainly to please Sally but also because he finds Laura's arguments logical and convincing. His curiosity is aroused, and he finds he is almost eager to put his detection skills, too long unused, into practice again.

Jake accompanies Laura and Sally to Max Laurence's funeral, and afterwards to the family home of Laura's parents, where he meets several other relatives and becomes aware of tension simmering in the air. The house is mansion-sized, and the family well dressed, but Jake notices the threadbare curtains, worn carpets and the washed-to-death table linen.

Figure 13. Part of a synopsis for a novel, 'Did He Fall?' © Chriss McCallum.

- The *first* two or three chapters (about 50 manuscript pages). Take time to make these as good as you possibly can – they must capture their reader's interest *from the first page*, as well as showing your writing and storytelling ability.

RED LIGHT

It's the mark of an amateur to conceal the ending. This won't intrigue either agent or editor – it will simply annoy them.

- Your author biography, a page at most. Include anything about yourself and your life that makes you interesting and potentially saleable as an author.

- Sufficient return postage.

It's acceptable these days to offer your novel to several publishers simultaneously (unless their entry in the annual reference books says they won't consider multiple submissions), but it is still customary to approach only one agent at a time.

Agents work on commission, making no money till their author does. They bear the expense of assessing the book and approaching publishers, and maybe also offering you editorial advice to help you improve your novel. Agents and publishers talk to each other all the time, and you'll be pretty unpopular if two agents find they're working on the same book.

Consult the reference books (the latest editions *only*) for the preferred method of approach.

If you can't interest an agent, or if you'd rather try approaching publishers yourself, get the name of the appropriate editor at your target publishing company. Call the switchboard and ask, and get the spelling right. Don't rely on even the latest reference books for this kind of information – editors move about too much for that.

And when you're eventually offered a contract, apply to join the Society of Authors. The *offer* makes you eligible for membership, and the Society will check out the contract for you *before* you sign it.

Here are a few tips about contacting agents and editors:

♦ *Do* address your letter and your package to an agent or editor *by name*.

♦ *Do* keep your letter succinct, to the point, and preferably not longer than one page.

♦ *Do* be professional. Your letter should be concise yet informative, and written in a tone that is confident but not arrogant or fawning.

♦ *Do* check your spelling, grammar, punctuation and syntax. If you send out the message that you don't care enough to send an immaculate letter, neither agent nor editor is going to trust you to deliver a competent manuscript of several hundred pages.

♦ *Don't* try to be funny – unless you're writing a humorous novel, in which case be very sure any wit you demonstrate in your letter really *is* witty, otherwise you could kill your chances there and then.

♦ *Don't* tell the recipient how much he's going to enjoy your novel because your auntie loves it and your best friend says it's the best thing he's ever read. Let the agent or editor make up his own mind.

♦ *Don't* attempt to tease by concealing your novel's ending. Agent and editor need to know you're going to deliver an ending that will satisfy the reader.

Recommended reading

Carole Blake, *From Pitch to Publication*.

Joseph Campbell, *Hero With a Thousand Faces*.

Dibell, Scott Card and Turco, *How to Write a Mi££ion – Plot, Characters & Viewpoint*.

James N. Frey, *How to Write Damn Good Fiction – Advanced Techniques for Dramatic Storytelling*.

Sarah Harrison, *How to Write a Blockbuster 'and make millions'*.

Nancy Kress, *Dynamic Characters*.

Betsy Lerner, *An Editor's Advice to Writers – The Forest for the Trees*.

David Morrell, *Lessons from a Lifetime of Writing – a novelist looks at his craft*.

Wood, Reed and Bickham, *More About How to Write a Mi££ion – Description, Revision, Setting*.

Now you should know:

♦ Your choice of novel types.

♦ How to check your manuscript's readiness for submission.

♦ How to prepare your submission package.

♦ How to market your novel.

10

Non-Fiction Books

Are you an expert on a subject that would interest a large number of people? Do you have first-hand experience or knowledge that might benefit, profit, amuse, intrigue or inspire others? Have you set up and run a successful business? Built your own house? Walked round the coast of Britain? Prospected for gold in the Andes? Perhaps you're already thinking about writing a book, but don't know where to begin.

In this chapter:

+ assessing your idea
+ first find your publisher
+ preparing a proposal
+ approaching a publisher
+ writing specialist non-fiction.

ASSESSING YOUR IDEA

Before you commit yourself to the project and all the hard work it will involve, ask yourself:

1. Is the subject big enough for a book? *An Encyclopedia of Houseplant Care* would be. *How to Water Your Aspidistra* wouldn't.

2. Would the subject interest a wide enough readership to make it a commercial proposition? Books do get written and published on some pretty obscure topics, but they're usually intended for a specialist market. It depends on how wide a readership you want

to reach, and on whether it's mainly profit or prestige you want. It also depends on finding the right publisher for your subject. Many publishers might want *An A-Z of Microwave Cookery*, but few would take on, for instance, *Advanced Theory of Semi-Conductors*.

3. Will the subject attract the book-buying public as well as library stockists? The biggest potential sales are in books on self-improvement (both physical and psychological), health, food and diet, leisure activities and hobbies. Do-it-yourself titles sell well, and books on cookery and gardening waltz off the shelves. 'How-to' books are in constant demand, especially those that show how to make or save money.

WISE WORDS

An American publisher, asked by a novice writer if he thought anyone would ever write *the* 'Great American Novel', advised: 'Forget the Great American Novel. What this country needs is a good book on how to repair your own car.'

You've got a suitable subject— so how do you tackle it?

First, break it down into manageable sections. The prospect of getting 30,000 words or more down on paper can be pretty daunting. Split into ten or twelve chapters of 3,000 words, it loses much of its terror – you can think of it as a series of articles.

Divide your subject on paper, then, into ten or twelve sub-themes. These will form your chapters. Under each sub-theme heading note all the information you already have relevant to that section. Note any obvious gaps in the information. You'll have to do some research to fill those gaps.

Now comes the crunch

Do you have, or do you know how and where to find, enough material to write each of your chapters *without waffle or padding*?

Can you realistically expect to pack every chapter with interesting and relevant information?

If not, abandon it, and look for a more substantial subject. Don't throw away your notes, though. You've probably got enough material there for several articles at least.

If you're sure you have enough material for a book, go ahead and prepare your proposal.

FIRST FIND YOUR PUBLISHER

> **WISE WORDS**
>
> Don't write your non-fiction book till you have a commitment from a publisher.

Don't write the book yet. If you don't find a taker, you don't want to have wasted your time writing an unsaleable book. And if a publisher does express an interest, he might want to make suggestions about the way you write the book – perhaps a different kind of treatment from the one you originally envisaged, or a format to fit an existing list. If you'd already written the whole book, you would have to do an extensive rewrite.

PREPARING A PROPOSAL

Make an outline of the whole book.

1. Set down your title. The publisher might want to change it, but for the purposes of the proposal you need a working title. Make it as snappy as you can. *Raising Funds for Charity* is more effective than *Organising Successful Events to Raise Money for Charitable Projects*. It would fit the spine of the book better, too.

2. Write down the first chapter heading, and set out underneath it, briefly, all the points you'll deal with in that chapter.

3. List all your chapters in this way, then juggle them into a logical sequence. This will give you the skeleton of your book, the bones on which you'll build the meat.

4. Type the outline neatly in single spacing, like a letter – this is a document, not a working typescript. An extract from such a document is shown in Figure 14. Indicate the proposed overall length of the book (its 'extent'). If illustrations are appropriate, say whether or not you can supply them. The publisher will advise you if he prefers to make arrangements for illustrations himself.

The sales pitch

On a separate sheet of paper, type out:

◆ A short, concise explanation of the book's proposed purpose and area of interest.

◆ Why you believe there's a need for it.

◆ What market you see for it.

◆ What competition there is.

◆ Why you believe *your* book will be better.

APPROACHING A PUBLISHER

Look through the publishers listed in the *Writers' & Artists' Yearbook* and *The Writer's Handbook* and list those who specify an interest in the kind of book you plan.

Next, check with Booktrust to see what other books on your topic are currently on the market, and if any are due to be published in the near future.

Overview: *Raising Funds for Charity*
The book will cover all aspects of fund-raising, from individual efforts (making and selling crafts, holding a coffee morning, hosting a sales party and so on) to larger committee-run business-sponsored events like dinner dances and concerts.

It will be spiced with accounts of real-life achievements – I know of a man who raised many thousands of pounds by hiring Concorde and flying a party to the USA – which will intrigue, encourage and inspire the reader.

Legal, health and safety aspects will all be covered. There will be suggestions for a comprehensive range of money-making possibilities, and a directory of contact addresses: services, suppliers, information sources and so on.

I believe that there are many people who would be attracted by having so much information offered in one handy volume. It will appeal to individuals and to organisations: clubs and societies, schools and colleges, hospital support groups, church groups and many more.

As far as I have been able to ascertain, there are very few publications on the open market that gather together so many facts and suggestions and combine them with an interesting and entertaining narrative.

And one of the essential ingredients for success in any enterprise is surely that the participants should enjoy the venture from the outset. The necessary literature should be part of the enjoyment.

Format:

I plan to structure the book in three sections. Briefly,

1. Setting up, forming a committee, and investigating legal matters.
2. Planning strategies and events.
3. A digest of fund-raising ideas.

Plus: Contact addresses, sources of information, useful publications and an index.

Figure 14. Part of a proposal and outline for a non-fiction book.

Part of an outline for a proposed book – *Raising Funds for Charity*

Introduction
A short general overview of the choices for raising funds as an individual, a small group, or a larger committee-run group. It will also draw attention to the need to know how the law affects various activities – to be covered in one of the chapters.

Chapter 1: How to set up a committee
Showing the various offices – chairperson, secretary, treasurer and so on – and defining each office and the responsibilities it carries, stressing the importance of allocating the right job to the right person. For instance, it's hopeless to appoint as treasurer someone who can't tell an invoice from a receipt.

Chapter 2: Fund raising and the law
What you need to know about what you can do without permission, what you need permission for – for instance, you can't sell raffle tickets door-to-door without a special permit – and what you can't do at all.

Chapter 3: Drawing up a provisional programme of events
Your committee needs to decide what is within its members' capabilities and what isn't. For instance, there's no point in trying to organise a jumble sale if your members are not prepared to sort out the jumble. It's no good, either, deciding to have a brass band concert if the nearest brass band is based a hundred miles away and you would have to meet its travelling expenses.

This chapter will include a list of suggestions for events: a summer fair, a Christmas craft fair, an antiques and collectables fair, a car boot sale, a raffle, an auction, a quiz night, a gala dinner and dozens more.

It will also point out the areas where you need special insurance and safety precautions.

Figure 14. Continued

Decide which publisher looks like the best prospect. Find out the name of the editor responsible for the type of book you want to offer, either by looking on their website or by ringing the switchboard. If the operator doesn't know, ask to be put through to the editorial department for non-fiction books. Ask there for the appropriate name, and check the spelling. Don't try to discuss the book on the phone unless you are specifically asked to do so – all you want is the right name so your proposal will reach the right person. (*The Writer's Handbook* gives many editors' names in its listings, but check anyway – publishing personnel move about a lot.)

Your covering letter

This should be brief and to the point. All the information about your book is in the proposal, so there's no need to repeat it here.

If you have any special qualifications for writing the book, mention these – but only mention *relevant* matters. Your degree in metaphysics won't persuade an editor to accept your book on fund-raising – it has no relevance. Your experience in the field does, though. All you need is something similar to Figure 15.

Dear Mr Corn-Harvester

I enclose a proposal for a book I am preparing about fund-raising for charity. I have 15 years of experience in this field, both in active organisation and in administration, and have published articles on the subject in *Fundraising Fun* and *Charitable Times* (clips enclosed).

Will you please consider my proposed book for your list?

Yours sincerely

Figure 15. Example of a covering letter for a non-fiction book proposal.

Prepare a sample chapter or two
You might have to wait a while for a reply, or you might have to try several publishers before you get a nibble of interest. Spend this time working on a couple of sample chapters and on gathering information you're going to need to fill the gaps you identified when you made your original notes.

When a publisher does express interest, he'll probably ask you to send him at least one complete chapter, to see whether or not the content will live up to the promise of the proposal. He'll also want to assess your capabilities as a writer before he commits himself, so you must make your sample as good as you possibly can.

When you're offered an agreement
If he likes your sample, the publisher will either ask to see the completed ms 'on spec' (in which case you should think very carefully before committing yourself to finishing the book with no definite prospect of acceptance) or he will offer you an agreement on the strength of what he has already seen. With the agreement, he *might* also offer you an advance against royalties.

The *offer* of a book contract entitles you to apply for membership of the Society of Authors, who will advise you about the agreement you've been offered, so as soon as you receive the document, contact them and they'll scrutinise it on your behalf, *before you sign it.*

Recommended reading:
Carole Blake, *From Pitch to Publication.*
Michael Legat, *Understanding Publishers' Contracts.*
The Society of Authors, *Quick Guide to Publishing Contracts.*

WRITING SPECIALIST NON-FICTION

The range of non-fiction books is almost limitless. If you have any kind of specialist knowledge, think about putting it to use in print. The following are just a few of the areas you might look at.

Educational writing

You don't have to be a teacher to write educational material. Teaching experience helps, certainly, in preparing course material or textbooks, but the most important requirement is skill in communication.

The educational writer has to work within strict guidelines. Content, language and structure must be geared to specific ages and abilities. You can get information about courses and relevant syllabus material from local education authorities, career centres and libraries. If you are a teacher you have an advantage over the 'outsider', because you're in touch with current needs.

There are openings, however, for those with no teaching experience at all. What you need is the ability to write well to specific guidelines.

English language teaching

The English language is taught all over the world, not only to children but to people of all ages. Most of this teaching is done with storybooks, not textbooks. Some of these are original stories, but many are adapted from modern novels and from the life stories of famous people – Marilyn Monroe, Charlie Chaplin, Sir Winston Churchill, Nelson Mandela ... Non-fiction subjects like airports, animals, earthquakes, volcanoes, the sinking of the *Titanic*, the Olympic Games and World Cup sport are popular, too.

What is required is a 'good read' to keep the learner turning the pages so he absorbs the language almost without thinking about it. These abridgements and adaptations have to be prepared within tight disciplines according to varying levels of ability. At the lower level, for example, you might work with:

- a given word list of, say, 300 words
- a given list of simple sentence structures
- very simple tenses.

With these as your basic 'bricks', you build a story or, for an adaptation, you use the existing storyline.

If you think you could make a go of this kind of tightly disciplined writing, contact publishers who have an English Language Teaching (ELT) department, citing any relevant qualifications and writing experience, and pitch a few ideas for stories and/or adaptations.

Reference books

These can be a good publishing proposition because they're steady sellers. There are reference books on every imaginable subject, from wildflowers to monastery sewerage systems. If you have an idea for a reference book – perhaps you've spotted a gap in the market – and have enough knowledge of the subject to write it, approach a publisher with a proposal as outlined on pages 112–16.

The religious press

Book publishers and magazines catering for all religious denominations need inspirational and educational material. Most of the religious publications in the UK are related to the Christian faith in its various denominations. You'll find publishers of religious material listed in the *Writers' & Artists' Yearbook* and *The Writer's*

Handbook. Many smaller religious groups publish their own books, papers and magazines. You're probably already familiar with the publications and publishers relating to your own faith, but you might not have thought of them as markets for your writing.

Whatever your religious persuasion, however, you should apply the same basic principles for successful writing: study each publication as an individual market, because they're all different and will look for material that satisfies their particular outlook and interests.

Most cities and large towns have at least one religious bookshop. You can browse there and look for the publishers whose books reflect your own interests. If you buy one or two publications, so much the better – you could then enlist the shop staff's help for advice about appropriate publishers. Your library, too, should have information on religious publications.

There's a society for writers of specifically Christian material, The Association of Christian Writers (see page 177).

Travel books

Successful travel writing involves much more than descriptions of journeys and exotic locations, or quoting from brochures and guide books. A travel article or book should:

- Provide insight into people's lives and culture.
- Create a sense of atmosphere.
- Bring a place to vivid life through details rather than generalities.
- Get the facts right, but treat them imaginatively.
- Be descriptive without being overloaded with superlatives, clichés and flowery adjectives.

Too many aspiring travel writers concentrate on descriptions of beautiful sights seen through the windows of their car or tourist coach. You need to spend time absorbing the local atmosphere, talking to the people, taking photographs and making on-the-spot notes of your impressions – not just what you see, but what you feel, hear and smell, what attracts, what repels, what arouses your curiosity. Dig beneath the surface, and be sensitive to the feelings of the local people.

If you need inspiration, don't turn to guide books or brochures – read Jonathan Raban, Eric Newby, Paul Theroux and the hugely successful Bill Bryson ... the best travel writers can transport the armchair traveller into the heart of another place, another culture. They make you feel the thin air of the Andes, see the grandeur of the Victoria Falls, smell the sweat that built the Pyramids, hear the echo of the jackboot in the streets of Warsaw.

Don't forget the photographs. They could be vital in clinching a sale.

WISE WORDS

Travel writing has more in common with fiction than with journalism. It needs more than facts, figures and descriptions – it needs the pulse of life. If you can achieve this, you'll delight the editors who receive your mss.

Copywriting

Copywriting for business can be very lucrative. The main areas are advertising and direct mail. To get a feel for what's needed, stop skipping the adverts and binning your 'junk' mail. Somebody has been paid to write all that material, and paid very well. Maybe you could do it, too, and develop a useful sideline or even a new career writing copy designed to sell products and services.

You could start by offering your services to local companies. Study their promotional material. Could you write it better? Can you think up a more effective approach? If so, let them see it. Present fresh ideas in sharp persuasive language.

Whether you're writing press releases, adverts, sales literature, newsletters, posters or TV and radio commercials, you need to know how to construct good copy and avoid the pitfalls.

Your writing skills could help small businesses in particular to promote themselves better and at less expense than could a large advertising company.

Recommended reading
Diana Wimbs, *Freelance Copywriting*.

Technical writing
To be a successful technical writer, you need many of the qualities and skills of an investigative journalist. You need to know how to sift essential information from masses of data, then present that information in terms that are easily understood by the people who need it.

To be a technical writer, you would need:

♦ To enjoy researching, possibly into subject matter you know little or nothing about, in enough depth to clarify the subject to people who need to understand it.

♦ To be skilled enough in human relationships to win co-operation from the people who hold the information you need – you might have to apply a little psychology when you deal with a temperamental genius (or even worse, with someone who thinks he's a genius).

◆ To possess a logical mind and a good memory.

◆ To be able to present your findings in clear, concise, unambiguous English, without resort to specialist jargon.

It's that last point that prompts many businesses to employ writers from outside the company to prepare sales brochures, users' manuals and suchlike. Company employees can be too close to the subject to see that what is commonplace knowledge to them might be a complete mystery to the layman or non-technician. If you've ever torn your hair out over a computer handbook you'll recognise the problem. An 'outsider' sees the gaps and the areas of possible confusion because he needs to get them clear in his own mind before he can pass them on to his readers.

And a brief look at some others

◆ Guide books – If you know an area well, either at home or abroad, you might be able to create a guide to help other people know it too.

◆ Biography – Do you have a special interest in and knowledge of some interesting person, either living or dead?

◆ Business and management – Do you have experience of some area of business that would interest others in the field?

◆ Computer handbooks – Can you unravel the complexities of computer and software usage so that the novice can understand them?

- History – Can you make people and events from the past come alive? There's a big demand for history books for both adults and children.

- Mind/body/spirit – A real growth area nowadays, with a burgeoning interest in alternative healing and the search for mystical knowledge.

- Personal finance – Do you have knowledge and experience that could help others order or untangle their financial affairs?

Now you should know:

- How to assess your idea
- How to prepare and present a proposal
- What a huge range of non-fiction books you can explore.

11

Writing for Children and Teenagers

Do you have a fund of ideas for stories, informative articles, games, puzzles, jokes and picture-stories? Could you write a 'young adult' novel, dealing with some of the serious issues that concern young people today? There's plenty of demand in the market for all of these.

In this chapter:

- ◆ writing for children
- ◆ writing for teenagers and young adults
- ◆ crafting picture-stories
- ◆ non-fiction for children.

WRITING FOR CHILDREN

Forget any idea you might have that writing for children is easier than writing for adults. It isn't. It's different, but it certainly isn't easier. Many a successful writer of adult material has failed in attempts to write for the children's market.

> **RED LIGHT**
> It's a big mistake to regard writing for children as a soft option.

There's no room for amateur attitudes here. Publishers receive shoals of stories with enthusiastic letters telling them 'My children loved this when I read it to them – I'm sure others will, too.'

Many of these stories arrive complete with unbelievably bad illustrations ('My friend has kindly done the pictures for you. She's always been good at drawing.') Unless your collaborator's work is

125

up to professional standard, this will kill your submission stone dead. Publishers usually commission illustrations from a regular 'stable' of artists whose work they already know.

Writing for children needs particular skills far beyond entertaining your own or your neighbour's children. You need to combine your adult language skills with the ability to get inside the mind of the child you're writing for.

And the younger the age group, the harder it is to cater for. The more simple and spare the writing, the more skill is needed to get it just right. When you read books on the subject by successful children's writers, you'll see what a complex discipline it is.

Read the recommended books, then decide if you could produce the kind of material publishers want.

Some teachers believe that many publishers don't really know what children like to read. They could be right, but to get your children's book accepted by a publisher you have to deliver what that publisher wants.

It's vital to study current markets. Many writers, especially older ones, tend to submit the kind of stories that were popular when their children (or even they themselves) were young. Their subject matter, language and treatment are out of touch with today's market.

Don't send work to any publisher without first making a detailed study of their products in the age range and type of book you want to write. Every publishing house strives for a distinct personality and style. Buy some of their books, get out your coloured pens, and analyse them down to the last comma. A vague notion of what the publisher wants will not be good enough.

Picture-stories, puzzles, jokes, comic strips

Look at the shelves of children's periodicals in the newsagents'. Buy an armful and study the variety of material there – most of what you see is freelance-contributed. Decide which ones you like best, then analyse them as you would any other magazine market, getting guidelines if you can.

There's a pretty fast turnover in new titles – not many achieve the long-term popularity of the old favourites, but it can pay to get in early when a new one appears.

Figure 16 shows how to set out the kind of picture- or photo-strip story popular in these publications.

There's a hungry market for puzzles of all kinds. You can usually find names and addresses inside the puzzle magazines themselves.

1 – Large heading picture. Leave space for title and the following introductory paragraph –

When Gary and Lesley Stark were orphaned in a road accident, they went to live at Springbank Children's Home.
Gary and Lesley hoped to find a foster family where they could remain together, but had been disappointed so far. One day, Mrs Martin, the house mother, had news of a young couple who wanted to foster the twins –

Picture shows Mrs Martin talking to the twins in her sitting room.
Mrs Martin – *Mr and Mrs Hardy seem a really nice young couple. They love children, but they haven't any of their own, so they'd like you to spend a weekend with them.*
Lesley – *That sounds terrific, Mrs Martin, but Gary and I won't build up our hopes too high. We've had a few disappointments already.*

2 – Caption – *But at first, the Hardys did seem to be the perfect foster parents –*
Picture shows Mr and Mrs Hardy, a bright looking couple in their 30s, smiling as they lead the children from their car up the path to a small, neat terrace house with pretty front garden.
Mr Hardy – *We've been looking forward to this weekend, kids! I hope you like our little house. It's going to be a bit of a tight fit with four people in it, but WE don't mind if YOU don't.*
Lesley – *It looks lovely, Mr Hardy, and we LIKE small houses – they're cosy!*

3 – Caption – *Mrs Hardy showed Lesley where she was going to sleep –*
Picture shows Lesley looking puzzled as she looks around small room with nursery furniture in it. The room has clearly been meant for a baby.
Lesley – *Mrs Martin didn't tell me that you had a baby, Mrs Hardy. This room is a nursery, isn't it?*
Mrs Hardy – *Yes, it is, Lesley. We did have a little baby of our own years ago, but she died, soon after she was born. We haven't had the heart to change the room since.*

4 – Picture shows close-up of Lesley looking thoughtful.
Lesley – *Poor Mrs Hardy. It must have been terrible for her, to lose her baby like that. Let's hope Gary and I will be able to help her forget her sadness.*

5 – Caption – *At tea time –*
Picture shows Mrs Hardy serving twins boiled eggs, toast strips and glasses of milk. She and her husband have meat and salad and teapot set in front of them. Lesley is sitting next to Gary, glowering at him.
Mrs Hardy – *Here we are, kiddies – nice eggies with toast soldiers, and lovely milk. If you're good, there will be stewed apple for afterwards.*
Gary – *What! B-but ... oww!*

6 – Picture shows Lesley smiling sweetly at her cross brother.
Gary – *You kicked me, Les. Watch where you're putting your feet.*
Lesley – *Sorry, Gary.*
(Thinks –*I had to stop him complaining about the baby food Mrs Hardy has*

Figure 16. A sample picture-story script.
Reproduced by permission of D C Thomson & Co Ltd. © D C Thomson & Co Ltd.

You could try jokes, too – children love these. Comic-strips are popular, too. Could you invent a character children would love – think Snoopy, Postman Pat, Bob the Builder!

WRITING FOR TEENAGERS AND YOUNG ADULTS

This is a constantly expanding market, with publisher after publisher launching new imprints to cater for teenagers and the slightly older 'young adult' market. There are great opportunities here for writers who can produce what these markets want. You need to be able to write with understanding but without any hint of condescension, condemnation or preaching. You need to like young people. If today's teenagers horrify, disgust or alarm you, if you regard them as alien beings, it's probably best not to try.

> **WISE WORDS**
>
> Don't try to write for children if you don't feel comfortable being around them.

Subject matter

Today's markets embrace many topics that would have been considered inappropriate for young readers not so long ago. Whether from their own or their friends' experiences, most young people today can identify with problems like divorce or a death in the family, single parenthood, homelessness, living rough, the 'generation gap', personal relationships, unemployment, shyness, trying to make sense of the adult world, etc. Stories about the problems of daily life as well as traumatic situations can help young adults to understand and come to terms with the darker aspects of life.

The markets welcome writers who can treat such topics with understanding and sensitivity. Read a few books in these ranges, to see if they interest you.

CRAFTING PICTURE-STORIES

Picture stories are stories told in picture form, either drawn or using photographs. The illustrations incorporate text as dialogue in 'balloons', and sometimes as captions in or below the pictures.

D C Thomson & Co Ltd are prolific publishers of picture-story magazines for boys and girls of all ages from pre-school to teenagers. They will send you, on request, a comprehensive pack of information about writing story scripts, and will encourage and advise you if you show promise in writing the right kind of material for them. (Enclose a stamped A4 envelope.) Send for the guidelines, and study the publications before you submit any material. Every magazine has its own characteristics, and you'll need to show an awareness of the specific requirements of any you choose to write for. Stories are not interchangeable among the magazines.

You won't have to supply the illustrations – they are done by commissioned artists – but you must present your script in such a way that the artist has a clear idea of what you want your readers to see in each picture.

The sample script (Figure 16) shows how this is done. It's a page from one of D C Thomson's girls' papers. You'll see that the speeches have to be very concise. There's no room in the pictures for long explanatory speeches. The text and illustrations work together to move the story along. And don't lose sight of the fact that what you're writing is a story, not just a series of scenes.

WISE WORDS

Don't offer stories that are patronising or 'preachy'.

NON-FICTION FOR CHILDREN

Don't overlook the possibilities of non-fiction. Think of the success enjoyed by the 'Horrible Histories' series, for example.

You need to be aware, though, that there are two distinct strands to children's non-fiction:

1. Trade non-fiction – the books and magazines that appeal mainly to the general market, the ones you buy from bookshops and newsagents. These range from the 'A is for Apple' books for tinies to teenage self-help books. Many trade publishers will consider ideas for books, but few will look at unsolicited manuscripts.

2. Educational non-fiction – mainly produced for schools and colleges. These range from language workbooks to history books and astronomy textbooks, and are usually commissioned to fit in with the school curriculum. Your best (possibly only) chance of breaking in here is through personal contacts and institutions like colleges and universities.

Recommended reading

Pamela Cleaver, *Writing a Children's Book.*
Allan Frewin Jones and Lesley Pollinger, *Teach Yourself Writing for Children.*

Now you should know:

◆ What it takes to write for children.
◆ What it takes to write for teenagers and young adults.
◆ How to craft a picture-story.
◆ The opportunities open in non-fiction for children.

12

Writing Poetry, Song Lyrics and Greeting Cards

Some writers have a natural talent for expressing their thoughts and feelings in a few well-crafted lines. Others have to work on developing the necessary skills. Whether you're a 'natural' or not, if you can produce inspiring work you can find outlets where it will be welcomed.

In this chapter:

◆ getting your poetry published
◆ how to set out a poem
◆ poetry 'on the air'
◆ where to get information about song-writing
◆ breaking into greeting-card writing.

WRITING POETRY

Poetry – the Olympic Games of writing. There's no money in it, unless you're lucky enough to win a major competition, yet the battle for publication and recognition gets keener by the day. Every poetry magazine receives thousands of submissions every year. Few have space for more than 50 or 60 in each issue, but that doesn't deter hopeful contributors.

GETTING YOUR POETRY PUBLISHED

Read other people's poetry

Writing good poetry is not just a matter of setting words out in lines, like chopped-up prose. Editors despair at the lack of craftsmanship displayed by so many would-be poets. You need to know how to combine the various elements of poetry to achieve the effect you want. The only way to do this is to study poetry closely, to analyse how its elements work – sound, rhyming patterns, rhythm and form, all have a part to play.

Research the market

Read what is being published *today*. Unless you're in touch with current poetry publishing, you can't know what editors are looking for. Too many poets are sadly out of touch. Some are still sending work of 'Prithee, I come my troth to plight' vintage to contemporary magazines. It isn't that editors only want 'modern' or experimental poetry. Far from it. Good contemporary poetry takes many forms. But editors still receive hopelessly archaic verse sent by poets who seem to have read nothing written this side of the Boer War.

> **WISE WORDS**
> Read poetry that is being published today — you need to keep up with the times.

Get to know the magazines you like, and support them

Every poetry magazine has its own distinctive flavour. When you find one whose poetry is in tune with your own tastes, concentrate on that magazine, at least to begin with. Don't even think about sending your poetry to a magazine you don't feel comfortable with, or in which you wouldn't be proud to be published.

Subscribe to at least one magazine, more if you can afford it. It's in your own long-term interest to help keep the poetry scene alive. You need these magazines as much as they need you.

> **WISE WORDS**
> Don't send anything to a magazine you haven't seen – you risk your poems appearing alongside others you might consider inferior or worse.

When you're ready to try for publication

Present your work as shown in the example below typed, single-spaced with the stanzas clearly divided, and only one poem, however short, to a page. Put your name and address on every sheet – on the back if you prefer.

Never send *anything* (even an enquiry) without an SAE. And please *don't* ask for free copies 'to see if I like your magazine' or 'to study your requirements'. Most poetry magazines are Small Press

---

Unborn Children

These ghosts haunt differently, they come before,
Slowly, like secrets, pointing empty sleeves
From the margins of life, and promise more
Than the pattern anticipation weaves;
Some day I'll hear their laughter and their cries,
Touch their small hands and kiss their sleeping eyes.

They sing their coming in a swelling life,
The pleasure of our bodies' creating,
A helpless immortality my wife
And I can only tremble for, waiting
Until we hear their laughter and their cries,
Touch their small hands and kiss their sleeping eyes.

They are my laughter at the frightened years
When pain was loneliness and solitude,
My freedom from my generation's tears,
A promise of a sure familiar mood
When I hear their laughter and their cries,
Touch their small hands and kiss their sleeping eyes.

Mike Pattinson

Fig. 17. Example of how a poem should be set out.
(*Unborn Children* was published in *Acumen* magazine in
October 1986, and is reproduced here in typescript form
with Mike Pattinson's permission.)

publications, struggling along on tiny budgets. Few make even a marginal profit. You shouldn't expect them (or any other market, for that matter) to subsidise your market study and your postage.

Saving money, time and aggravation

- Don't submit poems to major publishing houses. A few do publish poetry, but a beginner's work seldom meets their standards. Wait till you have a respectable number of poems in print before you think about putting a collection together.

- Don't send poetry to magazines that never publish it. They won't make an exception for you, however good you are.

- Don't send a saga the length of *Beowulf* to a small magazine where it would fill a dozen issues.

- *Never* send the same poem to more than one magazine at a time. This is 'multiple submission' and will damage your reputation. You risk a double acceptance – not the triumph you might think. Both editors will be embarrassed, and you won't be forgiven. Poetry editors see a lot of poetry magazines, and even if they themselves don't see your gaffe, you can be sure some indignant poet will 'advise' them.

Poetry 'on the air'

My thanks to Peggy Poole, prize-winning poet and for many years Poetry Consultant to BBC Network Northwest, for the following advice:

Outlets

If your local BBC or independent radio stations have no poetry programme, ask for one and organise area support. Poetry in the

21st century has a much higher profile than it has had for many years. Studio managers should be persuaded of this and alerted to the chance of a successful programme that will involve local listeners.

Submissions

Submit as for a top-class magazine, with an SAE. Keep poems relatively short – a rough line limit of 40. (This does not mean the total exclusion of any longer work, particularly of a possible dramatic poem for several voices. In such a case it would be advisable to write to the producer in advance explaining the content, and a decision will be made either to present an extra, one-off programme or to vary the style of the regular poetry programme for that one special occasion.)

Do not use four-letter words, even if they are an integral part of a poem; this will jeopardise the programme.

Keep off politics, and ensure seasonal work arrives with plenty of time in hand. Humour is welcomed provided it is genuinely poetic and does not belong in a comedy programme. It's best to avoid nostalgic or pseudo-religious poems – huge amounts of these are received, but hardly ever used. Religious poems belong to religious programmes, and one person's nostalgia, unless of real quality, becomes someone else's boredom.

A good poem should work as well on radio as in print, but it is important to remember that your audience is probably engaged in several other occupations while listening, so your poem needs to work instantly at one level while offering resonances of deeper meaning at the same time.

Study this market, too

Listen to as much broadcast poetry as you can. Details of poetry programmes are given every week in *Radio Times*, for both mainstream and local stations. Do listen, even if your work is not being broadcast that week – only by listening can you get the flavour of a programme.

Reading

Many poets want to read their own work, but studios at the average broadcasting station are usually too heavily booked for this to be possible. It will depend on the producer and the length and format of the programme.

Payment

Do not expect more than a token payment. Remember you are reaching a very wide audience.

Checklist for poetry submissions

1. Each poem is typed in the accepted form on a separate sheet of plain white A4 paper.

2. Your name and address should appear on every sheet.

3. You've kept a note of where you're sending each poem, so that you don't risk a multiple submission, and you've kept a copy of each poem submitted.

4. You haven't sent more than six poems at any one time.

5. You've enclosed a stamped self-addressed envelope big enough and bearing adequate postage for the return of the whole batch.

6. Always remember to keep a copy of every poem submitted.

Finding informaton and advice

The *Writers' & Artists' Yearbook* and *The Writer's Handbook* include information on poetry publishing, organisations and competitions. The Poetry Library (see page 179) will supply lists of poetry magazines, bookshops, and current competitions.

Recommended reading

Alison Chisholm, *The Craft of Writing Poetry*.
Peter Finch, *How to Publish Your Poetry*.

GETTING STARTED IN SONGWRITING

Do you dream of writing a 'standard', another *White Christmas* or *Stardust*? Do you watch the Eurovision song contest and think you could write something better? Maybe you could. From folk to rap, from traditional to pop, there's always room for a good new song.

You can't write music?

You don't have to. What you need is a collaborator. You write the lyrics, your collaborator writes the music, and you share any profits.

Look out for sharks

The 'shark' is the music business's equivalent of the vanity publisher. He asks for payment to write music to your lyrics. Don't throw your money away – no successful song has yet been produced in this way.

So how do you get started?

You can join a professional organisation, even if you're a beginner. You'll have access to sound professional advice and guidance. If you need a collaborator, you'll be helped to find one who will work with you, on equal terms, with no money changing hands either way unless and until your song makes a profit.

The Guild of International Songwriters & Composers is open to both amateur and professional songwriters. Services to members include:

- Free advice and song assessment service.
- How to promote songs to music publishers.
- Legal advisers.
- Publishing companies' names and addresses.
- Copyright of works.
- Who requires songs for publishing and recording.
- Collaboration service, songwriters' register.
- Song contests.
- A free quarterly magazine.

At the time of writing, membership costs £42 in the UK and £50 outside the UK. The society's website has all the information you need. If you can't access the Internet, send a stamped self-addressed A4 envelope for a free copy of *Songwriting & Composing* magazine, which gives information on the music industry and music publishing. If you have any queries about the society, phone or fax the Chairman, Roderick G. Jones, at the address given in Associations Open to Unpublished Writers (page 177).

BREAKING INTO THE GREETING CARDS MARKET

Greeting cards are very big business. According to recent figures, American citizens send out over ten million 'conventional' greeting cards every day of the year. And 'conventional' cards are only one category in a multitude of card types.

There's a rapidly expanding market here in the UK, too. Specialist card shops are springing up in every town. They serve a growing need: to help people express feelings they can't find the words to write themselves.

Take time to browse. Most of the words and ideas for the cards you see there have been bought from freelance writers.

Study the cards closely. While at first glance many of the lines appear similar, every company has its own style.

Could you write the kind of copy they use? Many companies print their addresses on the back of their cards. Contact them to ask if they issue guidelines for copywriters, and if they have any preferences about presentation. Some companies are specific about this, others don't mind so long as the ideas are laid out clearly. If there are no instructions, type one idea per sheet on A5 paper, putting your name, address and phone number on every sheet.

Half a dozen ideas are enough to start with. They might not buy anything from your first batch, but if a company likes your work they'll add your name to their list of writers and send you regular details of current requirements and urgent 'wants'.

Humorous cards offer the best chance of breaking in. They're the best paid, too. Here's one of my ideas bought by Hanson White Accord, reproduced here with their permission. (Most companies buy all rights – very few pay royalties.)

Mother's Day:

Page 1: You're a Mum in a million. Thanks for putting up with all the naughty things I've done...

Page 3: Good job you don't know about the rest!

Happy Mother's Day

This card, illustrated by a commissioned artist, won the 'Mother's Day Best Humorous/Cute Card' category in the Greetings Industry Spring Awards in the year it was published. It's a good example of a 'sendable' card that would appeal to a wide range of buyers. The judges said they 'could all relate to it'.

> **TIP**
> 'Sendability' is the key to success.

Payment
Payment rates vary, but most companies pay from £25 upwards (some pay £100 +) for each humorous idea bought. (Payment for other lines is a lot less).

Finding information
- The *Writers' & Artists' Yearbook* has a helpful section, giving advice on breaking into the market, plus a selection of company names and addresses.

- The Internet – key in 'greeting cards' and marvel!

Recommended reading
Molly Wigand, *How to Write and Sell Greeting Cards, Bumper Stickers, T-shirts and Other Fun Stuff* – a mouthful of a title, but a treasury of tips and examples from a former Hallmark staff writer.

Now you should know:

- How to get your poetry published.
- How to get started as a songwriter.
- How to break into the greeting card market.

(13)

Radio, Screen and Stage

Do you have ambitions to break into writing for the performing arts? There's plenty of scope. Radio and television in particular eat up material with an insatiable appetite. To break in, however, you need writing and marketing techniques different from those required in conventional publishing.

In this chapter:

- starting with radio
- writing for film and video
- writing for the stage
- getting your play published.

STARTING WITH RADIO

You'll have a far greater chance of breaking into television if you've already established yourself in writing for radio. Radio is the best starting point by far for new writers, especially new playwrights.

Radio allows far more freedom than TV. Anything goes. You can:

- Cast as many characters as you like, because the actors can play more than one part.

- Take the listener anywhere in the world with appropriate sound effects.

- Set your play against any kind of background in any kind of weather, in daylight or darkness.

WISE WORDS

Radio stimulates the listener's imagination – as the often-quoted 'little girl' said, 'The pictures are better'.

In television, all productions are subject to budget constraints.

Listen to as much radio as you can. Tape programmes you like and analyse them, noting, for example:

- How many scenes?
- How long are the scenes?
- How many changes of scene?
- How many players per scene?
- How many players in total?
- What kind of dialogue?
- What sound effects?

Note the names of producers whose work appeals to you, and try sending your script to them.

Finding markets

The British Broadcasting Company (BBC) is one of the biggest markets for freelance writers. Radios 3 and 4 broadcast around 500 plays a year between them, and with the coming of digital radio, new channels are opening up all the time. There are opportunities for comedy, drama, short stories, panel game ideas ... the scope is as wide as your imagination.

The best source of information by far is the BBC website (www.bbc.co.uk) where you can access 'The Writer's Room'. Here you'll find all the appropriate addresses and guidelines for script

RED LIGHT

You *need* these guidelines. If your script is not set out professionally, it has absolutely **no** chance of being read.

submissions, including the required script formats. If you're not on the Internet, beg or bribe a friend to download the information for you.

If you're interested in writing comedy, you can subscribe (free) to the Entertainment Writers' e-mail newsletter, and apply for tickets so you can attend programme recordings.

The *Writers' & Artists' Yearbook* gives a lot of information and advice on writing for radio and television, as well as for film and stage.

Recommended reading
Shaun MacLoughlin, *Writing for Radio* – full of wise advice plus examples of script layout.
Chris Curry, *Writing for Soaps* – many tips on breaking into this lucrative field, plus script layouts.

WRITING FOR FILM AND VIDEO

Most film and video companies will only look at material submitted through an agent. Once you have a track record of some kind, you could try approaching an agent who specifies an interest in this field.

TIP
You need to present some interesting works-in-progress, and preferably also a portfolio of published work. They won't be interested in a total beginner.

Recommended reading
Julian Friedmann, *How to Make Money Scriptwriting.*
William Goldman, *Adventures in the Screen Trade* and *Which Lie Did I Tell?*

WRITING FOR THE STAGE
Your best starting point is a local repertory theatre or amateur dramatic group. If you have no track record at all, it's unrealistic to

expect to see your name in lights in London's West End with your first effort. Not impossible, but not likely.

However, management companies send scouts to repertory productions all over the country. They're always on the lookout for original and potentially profitable plays, and yours might be spotted.

WISE WORDS
Never send anyone your only copy.

Unless you already know someone in the company, it's usually best to write to the producer first and ask if he or she would like to see your script. Give all the relevant details: type of play, how many sets, how many characters and so on.

Read up on contracts before you sign any agreement. The *Writers' & Artists' Yearbook* explains contracts in detail.

Playwrights groups
Ask your Regional Arts Office for details of playwrights' associations in your area. Most of these groups hold readings and can arrange for script criticism.

GETTING YOUR PLAY PUBLISHED
It's well worth trying to get your play published, especially if it's been considered good enough to be given live performance by a local company. You can send your script to Samuel French Ltd, who publish nothing else but plays. If French's publish it, they'll include it in their *Guide to Selecting Plays*, a substantial catalogue of plays intended for performance by amateur dramatic groups.

ACT ONE SCENE 4

(Into Daniel's fantasy) The stage remains in total darkness for a few seconds. Then we hear a voice off. It is Daniel's own voice but distorted and amplified to sound God-like.

VOICE: In the beginning there was the stadium. But the stadium was empty and the ground without shape or form.

There is a roll of thunder and a flash of lightning lights up the stage for a second. We see a deserted football stadium.

Darkness was everywhere. Then the spirit of God moved in the wilderness and said: Let there be light.

Lights up. But they are floodlights as at a football stadium.

This was the first day and it was good. But God saw that the stadium was empty and the gates were poor so he didst command: Upon these terraces let there come forth all creatures great and small.

Football fans enter. Bewildered at first. Newly born.

And he called these creatures *(pause)* fans.

Explosion of music. Cheering etc. It stops as suddenly as it began.

Then God blessed these creatures and said unto them: Go forth and multiply.

FAN: He said what?

VOICE: You heard. Go forth and multiply.

FAN: Right lads. Let's get at it. *(They try)*

VOICE: And this was the second day and it was good. *(Pause).* But not that good for he had not yet invented women. *(Groans from fans)*

FANS: *(Chant)* Why are we waiting? Why are we waiting ...?

Fig. 18. Example of how to set out a playscript.
© Steve Wetton. Reproduced with permission. From Steve Wetton's play *King of the Blues*, performed at the Derby Playhouse. Not yet published.

You don't need an agent to approach French's, but they prefer that the play should have been tried out in some kind of performance, because performance reveals flaws that might have been overlooked in the written work, and which you could correct before submitting the piece for professional consideration. They make no assessment charge. French's will send you, on request and free of charge, their mail order list of books and cassettes on all the media and performing arts: writing, acting production, make-up and so on, from Shakespeare to pantomime. (It helps if you can specify your area of interest.)

Theatre production companies

You could try making contact with some of the professional production companies who actively seek new writers' work. You'll find an encouragingly long list of companies in *The Writer's Handbook*. Choose those who invite new writing.

Now you should know:

- It's wise to start with writing for radio before you try television.
- Where to get information on outlets.
- How to get started in playwriting.

Self-Financed Publishing

Publishers do sometimes let a bestseller slip through their net, but they don't get it wrong as often as frustrated writers would like to believe. Many books are rejected because they're not remotely up to publishable standards. Many others are turned down because there is no ready market for them.

A publisher accepts a book and finances its publication because *in his judgement* it will enhance his profits or his prestige – preferably both. If your offering is rejected by publisher after publisher, but you still believe it has merit (or perhaps you relish the challenge of going it alone), you could publish it at your own expense – and your own risk.

Do take a very careful look, though, at what's involved. If you get carried away on a cloud of 'publication at any price' euphoria, you could be in for problems.

In this chapter:

- is self-publishing for you?
- beware the 'vanity' publisher
- what a reputable publisher does
- self-publishing options
- publishing your own book.

IS SELF-PUBLISHING FOR YOU?
Ask yourself these questions, and answer them with ruthless honesty:

1. Do you have enough capital to fund your venture? It will cost upwards of £2,000 to typeset, print and bind a few hundred copies of a very modest book. Don't offset sales against this – there might not be any.

2. Can you afford to lose this money if it all goes wrong? Be realistic – any such venture has an inbuilt high-risk factor.

3. Have you assessed the competition? What books on your subject are already on the market? Will your book be better? *How* will it be better?

4. Have you identified potential sales outlets? (Don't include family and friends – they'll expect freebies.) Is there *really* a market for your book? If your subject is specialised, do you know how to promote your book to potential buyers? Do you know where it would be cost-effective to advertise? Publishing a book is not difficult – selling it might be harder than you think.

5. Do you know how to prepare the copy yourself (or are you willing to learn)? Do you have proofreading experience? If not, you must add to your costs: typing, copy-editing (checking for typing and spelling mistakes, grammar, punctuation, syntax, ambiguity of meaning, errors of fact and so on), page design, typeface selection, cover design, and proofreading.

6. Do you have the time and stamina to go out and sell your product? Can you afford the services of a representative if you want to sell through bookshops?

RED LIGHT

Can you *really* afford to lose all the money you're investing in the venture? If not, *please* don't do it.

If you've answered 'No' to any of these, perhaps you should think again.

BEWARE THE 'VANITY' PUBLISHER

He isn't hard to recognise. 'Authors! Does your book deserve to be published? Write to

us ...' he sings from the ads in the national
press. 'Publisher seeks manuscripts, all
subjects considered ...'

What a tempting siren song it is, especially if
you're smarting from yet another rejection. But ...

Reputable publishers do not advertise for manuscripts

Why should they? They're knee-deep already. They can pick and
choose. And they choose very carefully because they're risking *their*
money and *their* reputation on their choice.

The vanity publisher risks nothing. He gets his money up front *from
you*, and he has no reputation in the business anyway.

However loud his protestations to the contrary, he'll give you *no*
editorial assessment, advice or service. He'll print your work exactly
as you supply it, faults and all. His contract will commit him to bind
only a small proportion of the copies you pay for, with an
arrangement to print more as orders come in.

What orders? There won't be any reviews. He is well known to the
book trade. No reputable reviewer or publication will promote his
products. No bookseller will stock them.

So where does that leave you? Out of pocket, disillusioned,
disappointed and angry. Left to do the selling yourself. And you
might not even have any books to sell.

WHAT A REGULAR PUBLISHER DOES FOR YOU

When a regular publisher accepts your book for publication, he will:

- Enter into a legal contract with you, detailing the terms under which he will publish your book, and giving full details of all rights and royalties agreed.

- Possibly (but not invariably) pay you an advance against the royalties you'll eventually earn.

- Arrange all the editing, designing, printing and binding.

- Handle warehousing and stock control.

- Arrange publicity.

- Handle all the accounting work.

- *Bear the cost of all the above.*

He'll do all these things to the best of his ability because *his* money and *his* reputation are at stake.

You won't have all this experience, expertise, organisation and finance behind you. You'll be on your own, and you'll be taking *all* the risks.

Be cautious about poetry, too

If you value your reputation as a poet, steer well clear of paying to have your work published by someone else. Avoid, too, those anthology competitions that have spread like a rash in recent years. No matter how good *your* poems might be, you'll have no control over the quality of the other poems selected. Your reputation could be badly tarnished, perhaps irretrievably.

Don't fall for these seductive advertisements. The risks are far too great.

SELF-PUBLISHING OPTIONS
Low-cost methods

1. Do the whole thing yourself, with a word processor or computer and a photocopier and a stapler.

2. Have your text typeset and printed by your local 'instant print' shop, and collate the pages yourself.

3. There might be a community press in your area, with printing equipment. Ask at the public library.

If you have a little money to spend

For a moderate outlay, you can have your poems printed and made up as booklets or greeting cards. Get prices from your local printer or investigate some of the printing services advertised in writers' magazines.

RED LIGHT
Make sure you're buying a *printing service, not* a publishing service.

Could you produce your poems yourself in calligraphic handwriting on parchment or heavy paper? Mounted in photo-frames, these make popular gifts and sell well at craft fairs. With a bit of imagination, you could have tea-towels or T-shirts printed with your poetry. Look in *Yellow Pages* for local companies who provide these services.

Could you provide a service writing poems to order, for people to keep themselves or give as gifts on special occasions like birthdays and anniversaries? You could offer a choice of frames or card mounts, all readily available from art shops or mail order companies – look in art magazines.

PUBLISHING YOUR OWN BOOK

If you're sure you can afford the risk, go ahead. Advantages include:

1. Your book gets published.
2. Your book gets published quickly.
3. Your book gets published exactly as you want it.
4. You control the whole editorial process.
5. You control the advertising and marketing.
6. You keep all the profits.

Of the books available to guide you through the whole venture and show you how to market your book, the best I know is *How To Publish Your Own Book*, by Vernon Coleman, a brilliantly successful self-publisher.

For poetry publishing, I recommend *How to Publish Your Poetry*, by Peter Finch.

Now you should know:

♦ If self-publishing is a viable option for you.
♦ How to avoid getting caught in the 'vanity' publishing trap.
♦ How to publish your poetry by low-cost means.
♦ Where to find more information.

(15)

Competitions

Competitions give you the chance to write the kind of stories and poems that can be hard to place in mainstream markets. They also help you develop self-discipline in writing to set lengths and in meeting deadlines. Look particularly for competitions that offer publication. Getting into print as a winner gives you more than a prize and an ego boost – it gives you a record of publication to add to your CV.

In this chapter:

- which competitions to enter and which to avoid
- what you could win
- what the judges look for
- how to maximise your chances
- where to find out more.

COMPETITIONS TO ENTER ...

Top of the list are well-established prestigious competitions like, for example, the annual Bridport awards for short stories and poetry, the Arvon biennial poetry awards, and the Crime Writers Association Macallan award for the best short crime story of the year. These competitions carry tremendous kudos in the writing world.

Look also for short story competitions in newspapers and in magazines. Several top women's magazines run regular short story competitions, and publish the winners and runners-up.

Many Small Press publications run competitions, often relying on entry fees to keep afloat financially. The better ones are well produced and have a healthy circulation. (See Chapter 8.)

Don't let fear of competing with well-known writers put you off entering big competitions. Entries are usually kept anonymous till the judging is finished. There are several ways of doing this, and each competition gives details in its literature and entry forms.

DID YOU KNOW?

Big poetry competitions are more like lotteries than contests. Usually, entries are divided among a panel of adjudicators. Each judge compiles a shortlist, then all the judges read all the shortlisted entries *only*. If a judge eliminates your entry in the first round, no one else will see it.

Each judge then selects a 'short shortlist', and the winners are chosen from these survivors – sometimes with a good deal of heat. Philip Larkin once said in public that his fellow judges of a major poetry competition had awarded the top prize to a poem that didn't make sense.

... AND SOME YOU WOULD BE WISE TO AVOID

There are plenty of competitions around that could be classed as 'vanity' publishing ventures. These 'competitions' invite entries, usually poetry, to be considered for publication in an anthology – only there is no real selection process. There are no losers. Every entry is awarded 'semi-finalist' status, and the writer is invited to order (expensive) copies of the anthology in which their work will be featured.

Here, for example, is a 'poem' I submitted to one of these competitions, as an experiment. This effort won extravagant praise and 'semi-finalist' status:

Blackbirds in Spring

Blackbirds are nesting in our eaves,
Feeding their babies with worms and leaves.
Till one fine morning
Without a minute's warning
They all got up and flew away to Africa.

Would you be happy to see *your* poem in the same volume – perhaps on the same page – as rubbish like that?

WHAT YOU COULD WIN

Publication is the most sought-after prize of all. Competitions that guarantee publication of the winning entries attract by far the heaviest postbag.

Most cash prizes fall somewhere between £25 and a few hundred pounds. They're worth trying, as long as the entry fee is not out of proportion. Even a small cash prize can help to fund other entries.

There are some 'biggies', though, like the Arvon competition, which has a first prize of £5,000.

WHAT THE JUDGES LOOK FOR

In short-story competitions, the same qualities a fiction editor looks for:

- A story that grabs and holds the reader's interest.
- A story that stimulates the desire to know 'what happens next'.
- A story that is soundly structured.
- A story that is fluently written.

Note, a *story*. Essays, personal memoirs, stories in poetry form, opinion pieces and so on are *not* short stories. Yet such pieces arrive for every short story competition – and are invariably eliminated.

Look at your entry with cool detachment. Don't submit a story that will cause the judge to groan, 'Oh no! Not *that* one again!' Here are ten plots that need a very long rest – if *your* story resembles any of these, think again.

1. The ghostly hitchhiker: heroine picks up passenger on quiet country road. Passenger vanishes, heroine staggers to nearby inn where gnarled ancient recalls local man's grisly end on that road exactly fifty years ago to the day.

2. Blind date: bored/sad/neglected heroine inserts/answers 'lonely hearts' ad. Surprise, surprise, blind date is equally bored/sad/ neglected and now astonished husband/lover; they clasp hands and vow to revitalise their relationship. Variation – couple on naughty weekend. Double meanings abound, till the last paragraph reveals them to be husband and wife.

3. The man in the back seat: heroine's car is chased by a maniac driver. She slews into a ditch, runs, pursuer catches her and lo! – it's her neighbour trying to warn her there's an escaped convict in the back of her car.

4. The prize-winning roses: perfect roses win local flower show. Jealous loser pokes around potting shed, finds case belonging to winner's wife (allegedly visiting sick sister). Grisly remains found under rose bushes. Variation: roses weeping blood.

5. Who's a clever boy then?: after heroic adventures/mischievous pranks and many coy hints, narrator revealed as Ginger Tom next door/Betty the Black Widow Spider/Billy the Bluffing Budgie ...

6. The lucky day: racing correspondent picks up discarded morning paper, turns to back page, reads that day's winners. Sure enough, the paper bears the next day's date, he wins a fortune, then gets wiped out driving home. Wind catches newspaper, big black headline reads: 'Well-known tipster dies in fatal crash.'

7. Mutual sacrifice (*pace* de Maupassant): hero sells treasured pocket-watch to buy antique comb for beloved; she sells her flowing tresses to buy gold chain for his watch.

8. Dreamtime: heroine has wonderful/terrible/amazing experience, wakes up – 'It was all a dream'. Variation: cyclical dream, opening sequence repeated at the end ... she's condemned to live the dream over and over ...

9. The far side: narrator paints himself into 'no way out' corner – 'And then, dear reader, I died!'

10. Genesis: two children survive the end of the world, grow up, have two sons, call them (you guessed?) Cain and Abel.

In poetry competitions, the qualities an adjudicator looks for were summarised by the late Howard Sergeant MBE, founding editor of *Outposts Poetry Quarterly* for over 40 years. Howard's criteria are reproduced here by kind permission of his widow, Jean. They are:

- Craftsmanship.
- Adequate command of tone and language appropriate to the poem in question.
- Individual vision and use of imagination.
- Genuine feeling and personal contact.

In playwriting competitions, judging criteria vary enormously because of differences in the facilities and economics of the companies organising them. Each competition should indicate its requirements in its literature, and it will be an advantage to familiarise yourself with the venue where the winning plays will be performed. You can then avoid obviously impossible special effects and staging.

HOW TO MAXIMISE YOUR CHANCES

The DOs

1. *Do* read the rules. That's obvious? You should see how many people don't bother. It's foolish to invite elimination – if you infringe *any* of the rules, you're out, and no one will return your entry fee.

2. *Do* write what is asked for. If the competition is for a short story, don't send in an article or a memoir or a true story or anything else that is not a short piece of fiction.

3. *Do* respect the stated word or line limits. The judges *will* notice if you don't, and will eliminate your entry. They are bound by the rules, too.

4. *Do* study your 'market'. If the prize includes publication, it makes sense to study the magazine or newspaper that will print the winners. Make sure your entry is appropriate. Explicit sex, violence or over-strong language would be unacceptable in a national women's or 'family' magazine.

5. *Do* keep a copy of your entry, whether you'll get your ms back or not (and most competitions don't return them).

6. *Do* stick to the standard ms layouts, unless the rules state otherwise.

7. *Do* remember that judges, like editors, are human (yes, truly), and could be put off by bad presentation. Don't send a manuscript with handwritten amendments, overtyped words, or patches of correction fluid. Reprint or retype if necessary. First impressions count.

8. *Do* allow time to check for misspellings, dodgy grammar and ambiguous syntax.

9. *Do* comply of you're asked to write under a pseudonym with your real name only on the entry form, otherwise you'll be disqualified.

10. *Do* comply if the rules require you to suggest a market for your entry, and *do* check that the market you name accepts contributions. You might consider your entry suitable for *any* market, but you must comply with the rules.

11. *Do* get your entry in on time. If it arrives late, it will be disqualified and you'll have done all that work for nothing.

> **WISE WORDS**
> Study and comply totally with all the rules – you'll be throwing away your entry fee if you don't.

And the DON'Ts

1. *Don't* enter *any* competition that requires you to surrender copyright. However tempting the prizes, you could be signing away long-term benefits. Your poem might become a favourite for anthologies or even school textbooks, your short story might be adapted for radio or TV – it might even become the basis for a series, and if you've given up your copyright you'll have no right to any payment.

2. *Don't* enter *any* competition without reading its rules.

3. *Don't* pack your entry in fancy folders, decorated cover-sheets, ribbon bows and the like. They're a nuisance to the organisers and will go straight into the bin. (I once received a padded envelope containing a cardboard document wallet containing a mass of

tissue paper covering a plastic sleeve containing a single poem.) Judges are wary of fancy packaging – it often holds the poorest entries.

4. *Don't* forget to enclose your entry fee. Nobody will send you a reminder. Your entry will simply be disqualified.

5. *Don't* be too devastated if you don't win. Try a bit harder next time.

Checklist

1. Have you read and complied with *all* the rules?

2. Have you written what was asked for?

3. Is your entry suitable for publication, if applicable?

4. Have you complied with the stipulated lengths?

5. Have you typed your ms in the standard layout, on one side only of plain white A4 paper?

6. Have you kept a copy?

7. Have you understood and followed any special instructions?

8. Have you completed and enclosed the entry form, if one is required?

9. Have you enclosed the correct entry fee, made your cheque or postal order payable to the designated name, and *signed your cheque*?

10. Have you enclosed a suitable SAE if one was requested?

WHERE TO FIND OUT MORE

1. *Writers' News* and *Writers' Forum* run competitions for subscribers, and carry news of other current and upcoming competitions.

2. For information about poetry competitions contact the Poetry Library.

3. The bi-monthly *Competitions Bulletin* carries information on current and upcoming competitions.

Recommended reading

Iain Pattison and Alison Chisholm, *Writing Competitions – the way to win.*

Now you should know:

- Which competitions to enter and which to avoid.
- What the judges look for.
- How to give your entry a fighting chance.

Glossary

Advance. Money paid to an author in advance of publication of his book. Under the usual terms the publisher will retain the author's royalty until the advance is paid off, after which the author receives his agreed share of the profits.

Agreement. See Contract.

Anthology. A collection of stories, poems and so on, which may or may not have been published before.

Article. A piece of prose dealing with a single subject (or possibly several related subjects).

Artwork. Illustrations, photographs, ornamental lettering, fancy headings, etc.

Autobiography. A person's life story, written by himself.

Biography. A person's life story as investigated and evaluated by someone else.

Blurb. Promotional text on a book jacket or cover.

Boxed item. Information supporting an article. Sometimes called a sidebar.

Bullet. A large dot preceding and adding emphasis to an item in a book or article.

Byline. A line before or after a piece, identifying the writer.

©. A symbol signifying that a work is protected by copyright.

'Category' fiction. Fiction written to fit a specific genre: mystery, romance, thriller etc.

Clip. A piece of published work cut or photocopied from a publication.

Collaboration. Two or more people working together to produce a work, sometimes published under a single pseudonym. (For example, Nicci Gerrard and Sean French, who write mysteries together as 'Nicci French'.)

Commissioned article. An article written to the order of an editor who promises to buy the finished piece at an agreed price.

Consumer magazine. A magazine covering general affairs, sports, hobbies etc. rather than business, trade and professional matters.

Contract. A signed document, an agreement between publisher and author specifying the exact responsibilities each party undertakes in the writing, production and marketing of a book, in terms of payment, assignation of rights and so on.

Copy. Matter to be typeset. Usually refers to the prepared typescript.

Copy-editing. The preparation of a typescript for the printer by a copy-editor employed by the publisher to check facts, correct spelling and punctuation, syntax etc., and possibly to rewrite clumsily written or inaccurate text.

Copyright. The exclusive right in his own work of an author or other designated party, as defined by law.

Copywriting. Writing material for use in advertisements, publicity, etc.

Critique. A critical examination and written assessment of a work.

Deadline. The latest date or time by which a job must be finished.

Desktop. The computer screen, where icons for programs etc. are shown.

Draft. A preliminary version.

DTP (desktop publishing). Computer programs used to design pages (text and pictures) on screen instead of pasting up on paper.

E-book (electronic book). A book stored on a computer file rather than on paper.

Edition. One printing of a book. A second or subsequent edition will have alterations, sometimes substantial, compared with the previous edition.

Editorial. 1. An introductory column in a magazine, usually written by the editor. 2. Text other than advertising copy.

Editorial policy. The editor's concept of the kind of publication he wants to produce.

E-mail. Electronic mail, sent via the Internet.

E-zine (electronic magazine). A magazine created and read on-screen.

Fact. A reality as distinct from an idea or belief.

Faction. Writing which blurs the distinction between fact and fiction.

FAQ(s). Frequently asked question(s).

FBSR (First British Serial Rights). The right to publish a story or article for the first time and once only in the UK. Not applicable to books.

Feature. A magazine or newspaper piece, an article that is not one of a series.

Fiction. Writing that is not and does not pretend to be truth, but entirely drawn from the imagination.

Flashback. Past action presented dramatically rather than narrated.

Folio. 1. A leaf, that is, two pages of a book. 2. A page number. 3. A manuscript page. 4. A postal workshop system.

Format. Size, shape and general layout.

'Freebie'. A slang term for a publication distributed free to householders, travellers etc. Anything given without charge.

Freelance. A self-employed person who sells his or her services or written work to a publisher for an agreed fee. A writer/journalist selling work to various publications but not employed by any one publisher. (Derives from the mercenary knights and soldiers who wandered Europe after the Crusades, hiring out their services and their lances.)

Genre. A literary species or specific category, for example Westerns, romances, detective stories etc.

Ghosting/ghostwriting. Writing a book in conjunction with someone as if it had been written by the other person, with no credit given to the writer.

Guidelines/writers' guidelines. Detailed specification of a publication's editorial requirements, terms etc.

Hack. A derogatory term for someone who writes primarily for money.

Hard copy. Copy printed out on paper.

Hardcover. A book bound in boards rather than paper or card. Also called 'hardback'.

HB. Abbreviation for 'hardback'.

Hook. A strong beginning to grab and hold the reader's attention.

House style. The consistent style in which a book or magazine is produced.

Human interest. Material about people, their achievements, problems, ambitions, social and economic circumstances etc.

Imprint. 1. The printer's name with the place and time of printing, required by law in many countries for papers, books and so on meant for publication. 2. The name of the publisher with the place and date of publication.

In-house. Work done or ideas generated by a publisher's or publication's own staff.

Internet. A global collection of computer networks with a common addressing scheme.

IRC (International Reply Coupon). A voucher sold at post offices worldwide, equivalent to the value of the minimum postal rate for a letter from the country from which the reply is to be sent.

ISBN (International Standard Book Number). A unique reference number given to every book published, to identify its area of origin, publisher, title and check account.

ISP (Internet Service Provider). An intermediary between the Internet and the user.

ISSN (International Standard Series Number). A reference number given to periodical publications, in a scheme similar to the ISBN system.

Journalist. A person who writes for a journal, newspaper, periodical and so on.

Justified setting/justification. The spacing out of words so that each line of text is the same length, flush left and right.

Kill fee. A fee paid to a writer when, through no fault of theirs, a commissioned piece is not used.

Layout. The overall appearance of a script or a printed page.

Lead. 1. A story's main character. 2. Journalistic term referring to the opening of a news story or magazine article.

Lead time. The time between copy delivery and publication.

Leader. A principal piece in a newspaper or magazine, a main story or article.

Libel. A statement, written, printed or broadcast in any medium, which defames an identifiable living person by holding them up to hatred, ridicule or contempt.

Literary agent. A person who acts on behalf of an author in his dealings with publishers, offering his work and negotiating the contract for work the agent places.

Mainstream fiction. Traditional or current literary subjects, as distinct from category or genre fiction.

Manuscript/s (abbreviation ms/s). The typewritten or word-processed paper text you send to the editor.

Market study. Analytical study of possible points of sale.

Mass market paperbacks. Paperbacks printed in large quantities by economical means.

Matter. Manuscript or other copy to be printed, or type composed for printing.

Media. Information sources: newspapers, magazines, radio, television and so on. (Plural of medium, i.e., 'medium of communication'.)

Modem. A device connecting a computer to a telephone line.

Multiple submissions. The same material submitted to more than one editor at a time.

Novel. A fictional prose story of any length but not usually less than 50,000 words.

'On spec'/on speculation. Applied to writing submitted to an editor on a speculative basis, i.e., not invited or commissioned. Also applied to work sent at an editor's invitation but without any commitment of acceptance.

Out of print. No longer on the publisher's list, i.e., no longer available except from libraries or second-hand book dealers.

Outline. A sketched-out structure showing what a piece will contain and in what order, but without detail.

Outright payment/outright sale. A one-time payment where the publisher buys all rights from the author.

'Over the transom'. American slang for the arrival of unsolicited mss.

PB. Abbreviation for 'paperback', a book with covers made of paper or card.

Photo-story script. A story told as a sequence of photographs with captions.

Pic/pix. Jargon for 'picture/pictures'.

Picture agency. An organisation storing photographs and/or illustrations and leasing reproduction rights.

Picture fees. 1. Fees paid for the right to reproduce illustrations in which the user does not hold the copyright. 2. Fees paid by a publisher to a writer for the right to reproduce his illustrations.

Picture-story script. A story told as a sequence of artist-drawn pictures, with dialogue shown in balloons, and perhaps with supplementary captions.

Piece. Jargon for any short piece of writing, whether article or feature.

Plagiarism. The use without permission, whether deliberate or accidental, of work in which the copyright is held by someone else.

Plot. The storyline, the central thread of a story with which everything that happens is interwoven.

PLR (Public Lending Right). A system of monetary reward for authors, based on the number of times their works are borrowed from public libraries.

Prelims (preliminary pages). The opening pages of a book: title page, contents etc.

Professional journal. A publication produced specifically for circulation in a particular profession, for example *The Lancet* (medicine).

Proofs. An impression or series of impressions of the typeset matter for checking and correction before the final printing.

Proposal. A suggested idea for a book, usually put to the publisher as an initial query, then as a synopsis of the whole work, with a sample chapter or two.

Publisher's reader. A person employed to evaluate a manuscript and to supply a written summary and report, to help the publisher assess its potential as a published work.

Readership. A collective term applied to the people who regularly read a particular publication.

Reading fee. A fee charged by an agent, magazine or publisher to read a submitted ms. Usually refundable in the event of acceptance and publication.

Returns. Unsold books sent back to the publisher from bookshops and distributors, for credit.

Rights. Those parts of an author's copyright which he leases to a publisher as specified in a contract.

Royalty. A percentage of either the cover price or the net receipts of a book payable to the author under the terms of his contract after any advance has been covered.

Royalty-free copies. Books sent out for review or given away for publicity purposes, authors' complimentary copies, or books returned from wholesalers or bookshops.

SAE/stamped self-addressed envelope. An envelope addressed back to the sender, bearing adequate postage stamps or sent with enough IRCs.

'Scissors-and-paste job'. A contemptuous term applied to work that consists of material 'lifted' from reference books, encyclopaedias, magazines and so on, rearranged and then passed off as an original piece of writing.

Screenplay. A film script that includes cinematic information e.g. camera movements as well as dialogue.

Search engine. An electronic 'catalogue', capable of storing hundreds of millions of website addresses, that searches out pages of material relevant to a user's request.

Serial rights. Rights covering material sold to magazines or newspapers. (Doesn't necessarily mean that the material will be printed in instalments.)

Setting. The process of turning typewritten or word-processed material into type ready for printing.

Shout line. A prominent line of text on a magazine cover drawing attention to an important piece inside.

Simultaneous submissions. The same material sent to more than one market at a time.

'Slush-pile'. A term applied to the unsolicited mss that accumulate in an editorial office.

Small presses. Small businesses, often one-person operations, producing publications ranging from duplicated pamphlets to bound books, of highly variable quality. Seldom profitable, and usually financed by their proprietors and/or other enthusiasts.

Stable. A group of writers whose work is regularly commissioned and published by a particular magazine.

Staff writer (US staffer). A writer employed and salaried by a publisher, as distinct from a freelance.

Standfirst. An introductory paragraph in bigger and/or bolder type summarising the content of an article.

Storyline. A distinct plot line, the sequence of events that keeps the action of a plot moving forward: 'And then ... and then ... and next ...'

Strap/strapline. An identification line at the top of a manuscript page.

Submission. A manuscript that is sent submitted to a publisher, with a view to publication.

Subplot. A plot thread subsidiary to the main plot line.

Subsidiary rights. A term usually applied to rights other than UK book publication rights. For example, film and TV rights, foreign language rights, serial rights and so on.

Syndication. The selling of the same piece several times over to non-competing publications, possibly in different countries.

Synopsis. A précis or condensed version of the theme and contents of a book, giving a clear outline and breakdown of the proposed text.

Taboos. Subjects, words, references not acceptable to certain publications.

Technical writing. The writing of company and product manuals, reports, engineering and computing manuals and so on.

Text. The body of typeset matter in a book, as distinct from headings, footnotes, illustrations and the like.

Textbook. Usually applied to a book written for the education market.

Theme. The subject of a story, the basic concept that links the narrative. For example, a moral concept – 'crime doesn't pay', 'love conquers all' or a specific human quality, like courage or self-sacrifice. Not to be confused with the plot.

Trade journal. A publication produced for circulation among practitioners and companies in a particular trade or industry, for example, *The Bookseller*, *The Grocer*.

Unsolicited submission. Work sent to an editor or publisher without invitation.

URL (Uniform Resource Locator). An address identifying an Internet document's type and location.

Usual terms/usual rates. The usual rate of payment offered by a publication to freelance writers.

'Vanity' publishing. A term applied to the publication of work on behalf of an author who pays someone else to publish the work for him.

Viewpoint. The point of view from which a story is told, the selected position of the storyteller.

Viewpoint character. The character from whose viewpoint a story is told.

Voucher copy. A copy of one issue of a publication sent free to a writer whose work appears in that issue, as a courtesy and as evidence (to vouch) that the work has in fact been published.

Warranty. The promise from author to publisher that the material supplied is original, does not infringe any copyright, does not include anything potentially harmful, and will not lay the publisher open to claims of libel or damages.

Word processor. A machine using computer logic to accept, store and retrieve material for editing and printing out in typewritten or printed form.

Workshop. A group of people meeting to exchange opinions and constructive suggestions on current work, usually under the guidance of a writer/tutor.

World Wide Web (also referred to as **WWW** or 'the web'). A network of graphic and text document 'pages' linked together on the Internet.

Writers' circle. A group of people meeting to read, discuss and possibly criticise each other's work. Differs from a workshop in that the work is usually done at home before instead of during the meeting.

Writers' seminar. A meeting of writers, usually with guest speakers, discussions, possibly workshops, where writers can make contact with each other.

Recommended Reading

Adventures in the Screen Trade, William Goldman (Abacus, 1996) pb £8.99.

Book Business – Publishing Past Present and Future, Jacob Epstein (W W Norton, 2002) pb £9.95.

Chicken Soup for the Writer's Soul, ed. Canfield (Health Communications Inc, Florida, 2000) pb $12.95.

Cracking the Short Story Market, Iain Pattison (Writers Bureau Books, 1999) pb £9.99.

Craft of Writing Poetry, The, Alison Chisholm (Allison & Busby, 1992) pb £6.99.

Dynamic Characters, Nancy Kress (Writer's Digest Books, 1998) hb £12.99.

Editor's Advice to Writers, An – The Forest for the Trees, Betsy Lerner (Macmillan, 2002) pb £9.99.

Freelance Copywriting, Diana Wimbs (A & C Black, 1999) pb £9.99.

From Pitch to Publication, Carole Blake (Macmillan, 1999) pb £14.99.

Hero With a Thousand Faces, The, Joseph Campbell (Fontana, 1993) pb £9.99.

How to Make Money Scriptwriting, Julian Friedmann (Boxtree, 1995) pb £11.99.

How to Publish Your Own Book, Vernon Coleman (Blue Books, 1998) pb £14.95.

How to Publish Your Poetry, Peter Finch (Allison & Busby, 1998) pb £8.99.

How to Write a Blockbuster 'and make millions', Sarah Harrison (Allison & Busby, 1995) pb £7.99.

How to Write a Mi££ion Plot – Characters & Viewpoint, Dialogue, Dibell, Scott Card and Turco (Robinson, 1995) pb £9.99.

How to Write & Sell Greeting Cards, Bumper Stickers, T-Shirts and

Other Fun Stuff, Molly Wigand (Writer's Digest Books, 1992) pb £9.95.

How to Write Damn Good Fiction – Advanced Techniques for Dramatic Storytelling, James N. Frey (Macmillan, 2002) pb £9.99.

How to Write Five-Minute Features, Alison Chisholm (Allison & Busby, 1995) pb £8.99.

How to Write Short-Short Stories, Stella Whitelaw (Allison & Busby, 1996) pb £8.99.

Internet Guide for Writers, The, Malcolm Chisholm (How To Books, 2001) pb £9.99.

Internet, The: A Writer's Guide, Jane Dorner (A & C Black, 2000) pb, £9.99.

Lessons From a Lifetime of Writing – a novelist looks at his craft, David Morrell (Writer's Digest Books, 2002) hb £14.99.

Magazine Writer's Handbook, The, Chriss McCallum and Gordon Wells (Writer's Bookshop, 9th ed. 2002) pb, £7.99.

More About How to Write a Miffion – Description, Revision, Setting, Wood, Reed and Bickham (Robinson, 1996) pb £9.99.

Oxford Dictionary for Writers & Editors, The, Ed. R. M. Ritter (Oxford University Press, 2nd edn. 2000) hb £14.99.

Snoopy's Guide to the Writing Life, Ed. Barnaby Conrad and Monte Schulz (Writer's Digest Books, 2002) hb £12.99.

Teach Yourself Writing for Children – and getting published, Allan Frewin Jones and Lesley Pollinger (Hodder & Stoughton, 2002) pb £7.99.

Touch Typing in Ten Hours, Ann Dobson (How To Books, 2002) pb £8.99.

Understanding Publishers' Contracts, Michael Legat (Hale, 2002) pb £8.99.

Which Lie Did I Tell?, William Goldman (Bloomsbury, 2001) pb £8.99.

The Writer's Guide to Copyright & Law, Helen Shay (How To Books, 2nd edn. 2002) pb £9.99.

Writer's Handbook, The, Ed. Barry Turner (Macmillan, annually) pb £12.99.

Writer's Market (Writer's Digest Books, annually) pb $29.99.

Writers' & Artists' Yearbook (A & C Black, annually) pb £12.99.

Writing a Children's Book, Pamela Cleaver (How To Books, 2nd edn. 2002) pb £8.99.

Writing Competitions – the way to win, Iain Pattison and Alison Chisholm (Writers Bureau Books, 2001) pb £9.99.

Writing for Magazines, Jill Dick (A & C Black, 1996) pb £9.99.

Writing for Radio, Shaun MacLoughlin (How To Books, 2nd edn. 2001), pb, £8.99).

Writing for Soaps, Chris Curry (A & C Black, 2002) pb £9.99.

OTHER PUBLICATIONS MENTIONED IN THE TEXT

The Bookseller, Endeavour House, 189 Shaftesbury Avenue, London WC2H 8TJ. Tel: 020 7420 6006.

Competitions Bulletin, Cherrybite Publications, 45 Burton Road, Little Neston, Cheshire CH64 4AE. Tel: 0151 353 0967. E-mail: helicon@globalnet.co.uk.

Light's List, John Light, Photon Press, 37 The Meadows, Berwick-upon-Tweed, Northumberland TD15 1NY.

The New Writer, PO Box 60, Cranbrook, Kent TN17 2ZR. Tel: 01580 212626. E-mail: admin@thenewwriter.com.

The Press Gazette, Quantum Business Media, 19 Scarbrook Road, Croydon, Surrey CR9 1LX. Tel: 020 8565 4200.

Quick Guides, The Society of Authors (qv).

Writers' Bulletin, address as for *Competitions Bulletin* (see above).

Writers' Circles Handbook, Jill Dick, Oldacre, Horderns Park Road,Chapel-en-le-Frith, High Peak SK23 9SY. E-mail: jillie@cix.co.uk

Writers' Forum, Writers International Ltd, PO Box 3229, Bournemouth BH1 1ZS. Tel: 01202 589828.

Writers' News and *Writing Magazine*, PO Box 168, Wellington Street, Leeds LS1 1RF. Tel: 0113 238 8333.

Associations Open to Unpublished Writers

Association of Christian Writers: contact the Administrator, Mrs
Jenny Kyriacou, All Saints Vicarage, 43 All Saints Close,
Edmonton, London N9 9AT. Tel/fax: 020 8884 4348.
E-mail: admin@christianwriters.org.uk
Website: www.aswin.uklinux.net/ACW

Bureau of Freelance Photographers, Focus House, 497 Green Lanes,
London N13 4BP. Tel: 020 8882 3315. E-mail: info@thebfp.com
Membership includes the annual *Freelance Photographer's
Market Handbook*, a monthly full-colour *Market Newsletter*
giving regular updates on all the *Handbook* entries, and access to
a highly efficient free advisory service.

Guild of International Songwriters and Composers, Sovereign House,
12 Trewartha Road, Praa Sands, Penzance, Cornwall TR20 9ST.
Tel: 01736 762826. E-mail: songmag@aol.com Website:
www.songwriters-guild.co.uk

Historical Novel Society, Richard Lee (Secretary), Marine Cottage,
The Strand, Starcross, Devon EX6 8NY. Tel: 01626 891962.
E-mail: histnovel@aol.com
Website: www.historicalnovelsociety.com

National Association of Writers' Groups (NAWG). Headquarters:
The Arts Centre, Biddick Lane, Washington, Tyne & Wear NE38
2AB. All correspondence should be addressed to Diane Wilson,
Secretary NAWG, Suite Two, 23 Cambridge Street, Bridlington,
East Yorkshire YO16 4JY. Tel/fax: 01262 609228.
E-mail: mikediane@tesco.net Website: www.nawg.co.uk
A UK-wide association of writers' groups. Accommodates
individual members.

Romantic Novelists' Association, Mary de Laszlo (Hon. Secretary),

57 Coniger Road, London SW6 3TB. Website: rna-uk.org

Society of Civil Service Authors. Contact: Mrs J. M. Hykin, 4 Top Street, Wing, near Oakham, Rutland, Leicestershire LE15 8SE. Open to past and present members of the Civil Service and some other public bodies and aims to encourage all forms of writing.

Note: The *Writers' & Artists' Yearbook* lists a wide range of writing-related societies, associations and clubs.

OTHER USEFUL ADDRESSES

Arvon Foundation, National Administration Office, 2nd Floor, 42A Buckingham Palace Road, London SW1W 0RE. Tel: 020 7931 7611. Fax: 020 7963 0961. Website: www.arvonfoundation.org

Arts Council of England, 14 Great Peter Street, London SW1P 3NQ. General tel: 020 7973 6517. E-mail: enquiries@artscouncil.org.uk The national policy body of the arts in England. Incorporates the English regional arts boards. *Live Literature* contact: Hilary Davidson, tel: 020 7973 6442. *Live Literature* website: www.liveliterature.net

Association of Authors' Agents, 2nd Floor, Drury House, 34-43 Great Russell Street, London WC2B 5HA. Tel: 020 7344 1000. Fax: 020 7836 9541. E-mail: aaa@pfd.co.uk Website: www.agentsassoc.co.uk

Authors' Licensing & Collecting Society Ltd, Marlborough Court, 14-18 Holborn, London EC1N 2LE. Tel: 020 7395 0660. E-mail: alcs@alcs.co.uk. Website: www.alcs.co.uk

BAFTA (British Academy of Film and Television Arts), 195 Piccadilly, London W1J 9LN. Tel: 020 7734 0022. Fax: 020 7437 0473. E-mail: deborahb@bafta.org Website: www.bafta.org

BBC (British Broadcasting Corporation), Broadcasting House, Portland Place, London W1A 1AA. Website: www.bbc.co.uk

BBC Writers' Room, 1 Mortimer Street, London W1T 3JA. Website: www.bbc.co.uk/writersroom

Booktrust (formerly the National Book League), Book House, 45 East Hill, London SW18 2QZ. Tel: 020 8516 2977.

E-mail: info@booktrust.org.uk Website: www.booktrust.org.uk

Samuel French Ltd, 52 Fitzroy Street, London W1T 5JR. Tel (general enquiries): 020 7837 9373. Tel: (bookshop): 020 7255 4300. Website: www.samuelfrench-london.co.uk

National Union of Journalists, Headland House, 308-312 Gray's Inn Road, London WC1X 8DP. Tel: 020 7278 7916. Fax: 020 7837 8143. E-mail: info@nuj.org.uk Website: www.nuj.org.uk The journalists' trade union. Membership includes the union's magazine *The Journalist*, which is available to non-members for a subscription of £20.00 a year (10 issues).

Poetry Library, The, Level 5, Royal Festival Hall, London SE1 8XX. Tel: 020 7921 0943/0664. Fax: 020 7921 0939. E-mail: poetrylibrary@rfh.org.uk Website: www.poetrylibrary.org.uk

Public Lending Right, Richard House, Sorbonne Close, Stockton-on-Tees TS17 6DA. Tel: 01642 6-4699. Fax: 01642 615641. E-mail: authorservices@plr.uk.com Website: www.plr.uk.com

Society of Authors. Contact: Membership Secretary, 84 Drayton Gardens, London SW10 9SB. Tel: 020 7373 6642.

Society of Women Writers and Journalists. Contact: Jean Hawkes, 110 Whitehall Road, London E4 6DW. Tel: 020 8529 0886. Founded in 1894, holds monthly lunch-time meetings/lectures in London, and has several active regional sections.

The Writers' Guild of Great Britain, 15 Britannia Street, London WC1X 9JN. Tel: 020 7833 0777. Fax: 020 7833 4777. E-mail: admin@writersguild.org.uk Website: www.writersguild.org.uk

The Writers' Holiday in Wales at Caerleon, contact D. L. Anne Hobbs, School Bungalow, Church Road, Pontnewydd, Cwmbran, South Wales NP44 1AT at any time with a stamped addressed envelope for details and a booking form. Tel: 01633 489438. Website: http://website.lineone.net/~writersholiday/

The Writers' Summer School at Swanwick, contact Secretary: Jean Sutton, 10 Stag Road, Lake, Sandown, Isle of Wight PO36 8PE, enclosing a stamped self-addressed envelope. Tel: 01983 406759. Website: www.wss.org.uk

Index